STOP
OVERTHINKING IT

*Because Overthinking Is Killing Your Vibe
- And Your Relationships*

DR. JOLENE CHURCH

Copyright © 2025
DR. JOLENE CHURCH
STOP Overthinking It
Because Overthinking Is Killing Your Vibe
—And Your Relationships
All rights reserved.

No part of this publication may be reproduced, distributed, or transmitted in any form or by any means, including photocopying, recording, or other electronic or mechanical methods, without the prior written permission of the author, except in the case of brief quotations embodied in critical reviews and certain other non-commercial uses permitted by copyright law.

DR. JOLENE CHURCH
Successful Thinking Publishing
Chico, California
www.drjolenechurch.com

Printed Worldwide
First Printing 2025
First Edition 2025

10 9 8 7 6 5 4 3 2 1

ISBN:978-1-958471-10-4

Interior Book Design by Walt's Book Design
www.waltsbookdesign.com

Core Colors™, Connection Compass™, and Golden Bridge™ are trademarks of DJC Consulting, Coaching & Training, LLC. All rights reserved.

For information on coaching, speaking engagements, or bulk orders, please contact: info@drjolenechurch.com

STOP
OVERTHINKING IT

Table of Contents

Introduction 1
You're Not Alone

PART I 5
Why We Overthink (and Why It's Getting in the Way)

    Chapter 1 7
    Overthinking Connection

    Chapter 2 19
    The Myth of "Perfect Communication"

    Chapter 3 37
    The New Belonging Crisis

PART II 55
The Heart of Connection

    Chapter 4 57
    Start with Curiosity

    Chapter 5 75
    Real > Right

    Chapter 6 91
    The Power of Being Seen

    Chapter 7 107
    Presence Over Performance

PART III 127
Where It All Happens

Chapter 8 129
The Workplace is a Relationship Lab

Chapter 9 163
Net-Weaving, Not Networking

Chapter 10 185
Conversation is Connection

Chapter 11 201
Styles of Connection

PART IV 213
Beyond the First Step

Chapter 12 215
From "Hi" to Trust

Chapter 13 255
Repairing Disconnection

Chapter 14 277
You Belong Here

Author's Note 291

References 293

About the Author 301

INTRODUCTION

You're Not Alone

Have you ever stared at a message for way too long, wondering how to respond just right? Or maybe you left a meeting and replayed a comment you made, over and over in your head, cringing just a little more each time. Maybe you've hovered over the "Send" button on LinkedIn, trying to find the perfect words to reach out, only to give up and do… nothing.

I've been there too. More times than I'd like to admit.

We live in the most connected time in human history. Our phones, our laptops, our watches - everything is designed to keep us just a tap away from each other. And yet… we've never felt more isolated. More judged. More unsure of where we stand with others. We're surrounded by noise, but starved for connection.

It doesn't make sense, does it?

Somewhere along the way, we started overthinking everything about human connection. We stopped trusting ourselves - and each other. We began editing ourselves down to what we thought was acceptable or "professional," instead of just being real. We overanalyze every interaction and underappreciate the simple, genuine moments that actually make relationships work.

And let me be honest: I didn't write this book because I've mastered connection.

I wrote this book because I've spent most of my life *chasing* it.

Growing up, I changed schools thirty-three times. Thirty-three. That's thirty-three new classrooms, new sets of names and faces, new social rules to learn, and new reasons to wonder if I belonged. I got really good at adapting - at reading a room, figuring out what people wanted from me, and becoming that version of myself.

But what I didn't realize until much later is that in trying so hard to belong, I was erasing parts of who I was. And when you spend enough time pretending, you begin to forget what being real even feels like.

So I did what many of us do - I put on the cape. The Super Achiever Cape. The I've-Got-It-All-Together Cape. The Let-Me-Handle-It Cape. And for a while, it worked. I climbed the ladder, took care of everyone else, led teams, inspired others, and built a career I was proud of.

But the truth?

I was lonely. I was tired. I was successful - but disconnected. From myself. From others. And from the life I actually wanted to live.

That's when I started noticing that nearly everyone around me felt the same way. From the C-suite to the classroom, from boardrooms to break rooms - people were craving something real. Craving to be *seen*. To feel like they mattered. To feel safe enough to just *be themselves*.

And that's when I realized: we don't need better scripts. We don't need shinier titles. We don't need more emojis or clever sign-offs. We need to come back to what makes us human.

We need connection. The kind that feels honest. Kind. Uncomplicated. Lasting.

This book is my love letter to that kind of connection.

It's filled with stories, reflections, and practical steps that will help you stop overthinking the small stuff - so you can start building relationships that actually matter. Whether you're reading this as a leader, a friend, a partner, a professional, or just someone who wants to feel less awkward in conversations - this is for you.

We're not meant to do life alone.

We're not meant to carry the weight of every interaction like it's a test.

We're meant to connect. To laugh. To grow. To repair when things get messy.

We're meant to be fully, unapologetically human - and still be worthy of love, respect, and belonging.

If you've ever questioned whether you said the right thing, or whether you're too much, or not enough…

Stop overthinking it.

You're not alone.

You belong.

And I'm so glad you're here.

Let's dive in.

PART I

WHY WE OVERTHINK (AND WHY IT'S GETTING IN THE WAY)

CHAPTER 1

OVERTHINKING CONNECTION

WHAT HOLDS US BACK: SELF-DOUBT, OVERANALYSIS, IMPOSTER SYNDROME

I used to believe that in order to be taken seriously, I had to become someone else entirely.

In the early days of my career, I looked around and assumed I had to be the most serious person in the room - but I wasn't even sure what that looked like.

Who *was* I? What exactly was my skillset? I hadn't followed the traditional path through high school or beyond. Changing schools so many times left me with one focus: get out. I was a good student - when I was actually present - but mostly, I just wanted to move on. Blending in to survive every day was exhausting, and by my senior year, I was completely over it.

On February 1, 1985 - my 18th birthday - I checked myself out of high school #32 and enrolled myself in #33: an adult education alternative high school. You probably know the type. It was the school where the so-called troublemakers went. The stoners. The kids who refused to conform to how society expected teenagers to act, dress, or behave. What struck me was that, despite their defiance, this group of nonconformists had still managed to form their own version of belonging - through their behavior, their clothes, and the way they showed up for each other.

And once again, I didn't fit in.

But this time, I wasn't trying to. I knew this was a means to an end. I was done trying to show up and fit in without fully disappearing - though, at times, disappearing seemed like the easier option. I was tired of the pit in my stomach. Tired of watching the tightly-knit cliques who had gone to school together since kindergarten, something I had only ever imagined but never experienced. I just wanted to get on with *my* life—the one I got to choose.

The truth? I had no idea what that life would be.

At the time, I was staying with my high school boyfriend and his mom. I had drawn a line in the sand with my alcoholic father and said, "I won't live like this anymore." With nowhere else to go, my boyfriend's mom graciously offered me a place to stay. It wasn't glamorous, but it was safe. It was mine.

School #33 became the beginning of the end. During my enrollment meeting, the school administrator reviewed my transcript to see what it would take to graduate. Had I stayed at my previous school, I wouldn't have graduated with my class in May - years of moving between schools meant I was missing credits due to different graduation requirements. Alternative school was the solution.

She laid it out simply: I could work at my own pace. The sooner I completed the coursework and passed the assessments, the sooner I could graduate. That was all I needed to hear. I loved learning. I just hated the social stress, the constant pressure to figure out who I needed to be in each new place - what I called the daily "social gut-ache." Finally, I had a way out.

I walked into the most non-traditional classroom I'd ever seen. Desks were arranged in a giant square, and students were working independently. There was no formal welcome, no teacher at the front of the room pausing instruction to address my late entrance. Instead, I was handed a list of the courses I needed to complete, the materials I'd use, and a space to do the work. The rest was up to me.

For the first time, I felt free.

This was my strategy: start with the low-hanging fruit. I needed some quick wins. In ten days, I finished everything.

There was no cap and gown. No family celebration. No flowers, gifts, or graduation party. But I had done it. I was out.

I thought that meant I was finally free from the pressure to fit in every day.

But the truth? I carried that pressure with me.

Without the school restrictions I'd faced as a teenager, I set out to build my life on my own terms. I found a job as a waitress, enrolled in the local junior college, found a roommate, and signed the lease on my first apartment. The girls at work were great - I finally felt like I had found a place where I belonged. It was the first time I had a taste of independence and stability, and I wanted to make the most of it.

So, I did what I thought I was *supposed* to do.

I over-enrolled in courses - seven of them - because that's how many classes I'd taken in high school. It made sense to me at the time. I had no mentor, no advisor, no blueprint. I was navigating life solo, doing the best I could with what I had. But balancing that many courses on top of work, homework, and paying bills for the first time was more than I could manage.

I didn't know how to drop a class. I didn't know who to ask for help. So I skipped some classes, got behind in others, and eventually, the overwhelm caught up with me. I ended up on academic suspension.

I was devastated.

But like I'd always done, I picked myself up and kept moving forward. I slowly started building a career - working in office management, bookkeeping, payroll, and admin roles. And little by little, I began taking night classes, trying again. At first, I chose the "safe" path: finance. It seemed practical. Serious. Professional. I even went on to earn an MBA. But none of it lit me up.

Because the truth was, I wasn't passionate about spreadsheets - I was passionate about *people*.

Looking back, I realize I spent so much time trying to fit into the mold of what I thought a professional should be. What I thought would earn respect. What I thought would make me "enough." I kept trying to align my education and career with what seemed like the right formula - but my heart always pulled me in a different direction.

I remember one of my earliest undergraduate classes - public speaking. It was just an elective, but it changed everything. For one assignment, I gave a speech so emotionally resonant that I made the entire football team cry. Every emotional appeal I'd learned in the course - I used it. Not for manipulation, but for meaning. For connection.

That day, I realized I could move people. I could reach them. I could *see* them - and help them feel seen.

And that has never left me.

Even now, whether I'm speaking one-on-one or delivering a keynote in front of hundreds, that same gift shows up. The ability to connect. To create space for people to feel something. To remind them of their worth and power.

But for so long, I overthought that gift. I didn't see it as valuable. I didn't know it was my superpower.

Instead, I kept trying to "prove" I belonged in leadership, in HR, in rooms full of decision-makers and data-driven thinkers. I assumed connection wasn't serious enough. That being able to make people feel wasn't professional enough.

I spent years trying to *earn* the very thing I already had.

And that's what overthinking does - it convinces us that what comes naturally couldn't possibly be enough.

In the workplace. In leadership. In rooms where I tried to "read the crowd" and figure out who they needed me to be - I was still showing up as a version of myself I thought would be accepted, taken seriously, and respected.

I became the most analytical, over-the-top overachieving person in the room. I thought being "professional" meant never showing that I didn't know something. I tried to be it all, do it all, know it all. I mimicked the analysts and leaders I believed had it figured out. I shaped myself into what I assumed leadership looked like.

I didn't realize I was already leading.

I didn't realize that connection - not perfection - was my actual superpower.

But I was too busy overthinking everything to see it.

Every meeting, every email, every decision - I was stuck in my own head, questioning whether I was doing enough, saying the right thing, or being taken seriously. I felt like I had to prove I belonged in the role I had already earned. Even after becoming an HR Director, I still wondered: *Do I really know what I'm doing? Who am I to lead these people? What if they find out I'm not as confident as I look?*

That, my friend, is the voice of imposter syndrome.

And it's louder than you think.

It's not just about doubting your qualifications. It's the inner critic that whispers: *Don't speak up. Don't reach out. Don't let them see the real you.* It's the voice that convinces you connection has to be hard, awkward, or reserved only for the people who've got it all figured out.

We think we have to be *more* or *do more* to be worthy of meaningful connection. So we overthink every interaction, over-prepare for simple conversations, and overanalyze the tiniest details. We armor up with what we think people want to see - competence, professionalism, confidence — while hiding the messy, authentic parts of ourselves that are actually the most relatable.

And in doing that, we unintentionally create distance.

From others.

And from ourselves.

The truth is, people don't connect with the version of you that's perfectly curated. They connect with the one who's real. The one who's willing to admit they don't know everything, who asks the awkward questions, who laughs a little too loud sometimes, or shares that they're nervous before a big presentation.

I didn't always know HR was where I belonged.

When I first stumbled into the world of HR, it wasn't because I had a plan - it was because the work needed to be done.

There was no moment where someone pointed to me and said, "You'd be great in HR." I just started doing the work - payroll, training, onboarding, classification and compensation, negotiations - because it needed to be done. It felt like administration with a human twist. And I knew how to get things done.

But slowly, something started to shift.

I found myself drawn to the *people* side of the work. Not just the paperwork, the policies, or the protocols - but the *conversations*. The coaching. The crisis moments. The quiet "Do you have a minute?" drop-ins. I saw the power of being present when someone was having a hard day, or when a conflict needed resolving, or when a leader wasn't sure how to connect with their team.

And strangely enough, I felt most myself in those moments.

At first, I didn't realize that the very things I'd spent years overthinking - my instinct to connect, to listen, to feel deeply - were the exact things that made me effective. I thought being a people person made me *less* professional. I thought my empathy needed to be hidden under layers of logic and spreadsheets. But again and again, the moments that made the biggest difference weren't the ones where I had the perfect answer - they were the ones where I *showed up as me*.

That's when it hit me: this wasn't just a job.

This was my lane.

Not because I knew all the labor laws by heart or could recite policy in my sleep—though I learned all that, too. It was because I cared. I *saw* people. I could hold space in hard conversations. I could bridge gaps and rebuild trust. I could advocate for both the individual and the organization—*and mean it*.

Human Resources. It's right there in the name.

I stopped overthinking my value when I realized my greatest strength wasn't in knowing everything - it was in *being* with people through anything. I could finally see what others had seen in me all along: that HR wasn't just a role I'd grown into - it was a reflection of who I am at my core.

And that changed everything.

But don't just take my word for it.

I've worked with leaders, professionals, parents, and students from every walk of life - and you know what I hear, over and over again?

Different stories, same fear: *If I show up real, will it be enough?*

"I don't want to bother them."

"I rewrote the message five times before I just deleted it."

"I didn't speak up in the meeting because I wasn't 100% sure I was right."

"I always feel like I'm one mistake away from being exposed."

Sound familiar?

We all do it. We overthink the message we want to send. The thing we want to say. The part of ourselves we want to share. And the more we overthink it, the more we pull back, over-polish, or stay silent altogether.

We think we're the only ones second-guessing. But we're not.

We think other people don't struggle with connection. But they do.

Here's the thing: Everyone's human. Everyone wants to feel valued, seen, and heard. We're just all a little scared to go first.

But what if *you* went first?

What if you showed up without the script or the polish, and just offered something real?

Not perfect. Just *real.*

That's what this book is about.

Not networking. Not schmoozing. Not faking your way through it.

It's about showing up, seeing others, and letting yourself *be seen.*

You don't need to be more.

You just need to be *you.*

STOP Overthinking It

Pause. Reflect. Apply.

What to Remember

- You don't need to become someone else to be taken seriously.
- Overthinking is often rooted in self-doubt, not reality.
- Connection isn't built on perfection—it's built on presence.
- Imposter syndrome convinces you to hide the very qualities that make you effective.
- People connect with authenticity, not polish.
- You are already enough to lead, to belong, and to build meaningful relationships.

Self-Reflection

Take a moment to sit with these questions. Write them down. Speak them out loud. Let them sink in.

1. When do I feel most like I'm performing or proving myself in relationships?
2. Where in my life or work do I overthink simple interactions?
3. What version of myself do I show the world—and what part of me do I hold back?
4. Who in my life makes me feel safe to be fully myself? What do they do that makes me feel that way?
5. What might happen if I showed up 5% more real in just one area of my life?

Try This Strategy

The 5% Rule

You don't need to flip your whole identity overnight. Start small. Choose one meeting, one conversation, one email this week and ask:

"How can I show up 5% more real here?"

That might mean:

- Admitting you don't know something
- Asking a deeper question
- Dropping the overly formal language in a message
- Sharing something personal or honest in a professional setting

Tiny shifts create space for authentic connection - and help you build trust without overthinking every move. **Over time, 5% adds up!**

Conversation Starter

Want to begin creating more connection with others? Try this one-on-one or with a team:

"What's something you used to overthink that you've learned to let go of?"

It's a question that invites honesty, lightness, and real talk—all without putting anyone on the spot.

Chapter 2

The Myth of "Perfect Communication"
Why Connection Doesn't Require Flawless Execution - Just Honest Effort.

If there's one myth that needs to be retired immediately, it's this one:

You have to say it perfectly for it to be meaningful.

This belief keeps more people quiet than anything else I've seen in my years of working with leaders, teams, and individuals. We hold back ideas, pause before offering input, or completely avoid hard conversations - all because we're afraid we won't say it just right.

And yet, the best connections in my life - and probably in yours - have come from moments that were *imperfect*, but *real*.

Some of the most meaningful things I've ever said didn't come out eloquent. They came out *honest*. I've stumbled over my words, backtracked, said, "Wait, let me try that again," and still built deep trust with people - because they could feel that I meant it.

It's the intentionality of sticking with it, desiring to make sure the desired message in your head is received in the way intended that makes a real difference. It's the focus on ensuring that others know they are valued and heard.

People don't need perfection.

They need presence.

They need effort.

They need to *feel you* in the moment - not be dazzled by a flawless monologue.

And yet, we put so much pressure on ourselves to deliver just the right message in just the right way, that we often end up saying nothing at all. We rehearse texts in our head that never get sent. We write long emails we delete before hitting "send." We replay a comment we made in a meeting on loop, worried it came off wrong.

Communication isn't a performance. It's a relationship.

And relationships are messy. They evolve. They grow. Sometimes they misfire - and then we clarify, repair, and reconnect.

That's what makes them real.

In fact, research shows that conversational, imperfect communication often builds more trust than polished, scripted messaging. A Harvard Business Review study found that organizations with strong "organizational conversations" - open, two-way, often messy communication - had higher levels of trust and engagement than those with rigid corporate messaging [6].

When we buy into the myth of perfect communication, we do something dangerous: we prioritize image over intimacy. We become more concerned with how we appear than how we connect. And slowly, that polish creates distance.

Believe me, I became a master chameleon. I knew how to say just the right thing to fit in. I learned how to deliver the perfect comment, the expected feedback, the professional response. I wanted to be impressive. Polished. Respected. But the whole time, I was clueless about how to just be *me* - how to speak my truth, share my perspective, or just be real in the moment.

Here's the truth: people will forget your exact words. They'll remember how you made them feel. They'll remember whether they felt heard, respected, safe, and seen. And none of that requires a script.

It requires simple things - like asking how someone's day is going and really listening to the answer. It means being curious about the person in front of you. What are their dreams? What did they want to be when they were a kid? What are they proud of? What are they afraid of? What gets them excited to get out of bed in the morning?

Because relationships take work. And communication is the heartbeat of that work.

Imagine going on a first date. You and your date choose a lovely restaurant - not too loud, not overly romantic, just a safe, neutral place to get to know one another. You're seated. Menus open. And then… silence. You both bury yourselves in the wine list or pretend to study the menu like your life depends on it. Your brain starts spinning: *What do I say? What's a safe topic? Should I compliment them? Ask a question? Say something funny?*

Before you can decide, the server arrives. Gratefully, you default to the easiest escape: "Are there any specials?"

They launch into a well-rehearsed monologue. You order the steak. Your date orders the pasta. Crisis averted.

As the server leaves, another drops off a bread basket. You both lean in, buttering a slice like it's your lifeline. Still no conversation. You chew in silence.

Internally, the monologues begin:

He must not like me. He's not talking.

She must not be into me. She hasn't said a word.

Self-doubt creeps in. The silence grows louder.

Sometimes, the best connections start with a little awkward honesty and a whole lot of heart.

Then - relief! The food arrives. Now there's a legitimate reason for not talking. And of course, no one wants to be rude and talk with their mouth full, right?

You can see where this is going.

Nowhere.

Two people, both wanting connection. Both wondering what to say. Both waiting for the *perfect* opening line.

But there is no perfect line. There's just *starting*.

The date didn't fail because you didn't have something brilliant to say. It failed because neither of you felt safe enough to be yourselves. Because perfection got in the way of presence.

That's what happens every day - not just on first dates, but in team meetings, hallway conversations, emails, text threads, and Zoom calls. We hold back. We wait for the perfect opener, the right moment, the ideal words. And while we wait, connection slips away.

We talk ourselves out of reaching out to a colleague.

We overthink replying to a message from someone we admire.

We edit and re-edit an email until the voice that once sounded like us gets buried under "professional" jargon and phrases we found on a Google template.

And you know what's underneath it all?

Fear.

Fear of being misunderstood.

Fear of looking stupid.

Fear of saying too much - or not enough.

Fear of being rejected when we finally show our real selves.

So, we trade vulnerability for polish. We swap honesty for efficiency. We weigh our words instead of honoring their meaning. And we wonder why we still feel disconnected - even when we're saying all the "right" things.

But here's the secret: *Connection doesn't need the perfect words - it needs the honest ones.*

The imperfect, messy, sometimes awkward moments are what open the door. The stumbling is what makes it human. And when we finally give ourselves permission to speak from where we are - instead of where we think we "should" be - that's when people lean in.

That's when trust starts to build.

Because real connection doesn't require you to impress.

It only asks you to *show up*.

I've coached countless leaders who've spent hours obsessing over how to say the right thing in a tough conversation - especially when it comes to feedback. They'll script it, practice it, stress over it. And then, in the moment, they freeze. They get so caught up trying to sound "right" that they forget to just be real.

What works - *every single time* - is when they drop the script and speak from the heart.

"I don't know if I'm going to say this perfectly, but I care enough to try..."

"This might come out awkwardly, but I want to talk about something that matters..."

"This is hard for me, and I don't want to get it wrong, but I want us to be better because of this conversation..."

Do you feel that?

That's honesty. That's humility. That's presence. And that's what people respond to - not polish, not performance, but sincerity.

That level of humility and intention *connects.*

Because it's not the words. It's the willingness.

Because communication isn't about the perfect delivery.

It's about meaningful connection.

And the most meaningful words are rarely the prettiest.

They're the *truest.*

Connection Over Correction

One of the quickest ways we disrupt connection is by trying too hard to *get it right*.

We worry so much about saying things the "correct" way that we lose the thread of what we were trying to say in the first place. We get caught up in tone, delivery, and word choice - so much so that we forget what really matters: the *intention* behind our words.

We worry so much about saying things the "correct" way that we forget the whole point of communication is to *connect*. Not to impress. Not to be flawless. But to reach someone. To let them in. To let ourselves be seen.

We start to share something from the heart, then stop ourselves halfway through and say,

"Ugh, I'm not saying this right - never mind."

"Forget it, that sounded better in my head."

"I know this might be stupid, but…"

We second-guess a joke we made and follow it with, *"Sorry, I didn't mean that - never mind."*

We interrupt a moment of vulnerability with, *"Does that even make sense? I'm rambling."*

We start sharing something real and then pull it back with, *"Forget it. It's stupid."*

We correct ourselves before we've even given anyone a chance to receive us. And when we do that, we teach others to do the same - to hide, edit, shrink.

We preface, apologize, and self-correct so much that the real message gets buried. Not because we didn't care, but because we were trying too hard to *control* the moment instead of *being in it.*

We fall into the trap of performance again - this time not to impress, but to avoid discomfort. We think, *If I can say it perfectly, maybe I won't be misunderstood. Maybe I won't be judged. Maybe I won't sound weak or awkward or emotional or too much.*

But in doing that, we disconnect.

We stop ourselves before anyone else even has a chance to respond.

We shrink instead of share.

We aim for precision instead of presence.

We correct instead of connect.

This happens at work constantly. A team member hesitates to share an idea. They have an idea, but worries it's not fully formed, so they stay silent. A leader backs off from giving feedback. A manager wants to address an issue, but spends so much time rehearsing how to say it *just right* that they lose the courage to bring it up at all. A new employee stays silent in meetings. Not because they have nothing to say - but because they're afraid of saying it *wrong.* A colleague sends a carefully crafted message that sounds nothing like their actual voice—and wonders why it didn't land.

Here's the truth: Nobody's listening for perfection. They're listening for *presence.* For effort. For humanity.

They're listening for *honesty.*

They want to know you care. That you're trying. That you're *there.*

The person across from you doesn't need a flawless pitch. They need to know you're trying. That you're sincere. That your words are coming from a place of care - not ego, not fear, not pretense.

A clunky but heartfelt message is always more powerful than a perfectly worded one that feels cold or rehearsed.

People connect with your *humanness,* not your flawlessness.

That means:

You don't have to say it all the right way.

You don't need a script.

You're allowed to pause mid-sentence and say, "Let me try that again."

You're allowed to be a person.

And when you do that—when you speak from a place of clarity and care, even if it's messy—something beautiful happens: people listen differently. They soften. They open. They feel safe.

So the next time you catch yourself overcorrecting or overthinking your words, pause for just a moment—and try this:

Take a breath.

Come back to the heart of what you were trying to say.

And say it simply. Honestly. Imperfectly.

Because that's where the connection lives.

We can stop fumbling for the perfect phrase by remembering that connection always wins over correction. This means that instead of overthinking it, we:

Say it anyway.

Say it messy.

Say it like you mean it.

Because you do.

What They Really Want From You

Here's something we don't talk about enough: most people don't need you to be impressive - they need you to be *clear*, *kind*, and *consistent*.

That's it.

We spend so much energy trying to craft the perfect email opener, make a meeting contribution sound polished, or deliver feedback with just the right amount of corporate finesse that we forget: no one is scoring us. People aren't looking for performance. They're looking for something they can trust.

They simply want to know:

Do you mean what you say?

Are you showing up with respect and care?

Will you follow through?

That's what makes communication land. Not big words. Not clever analogies. Not sounding like a TED Talk. Just *being real* and *following through*.

Think about the best communicators you've known - not the most eloquent or charismatic, but the ones who left an impact. They probably had three things in common: 1) they were present; 2) they were honest; and 3) they followed through.

They were present. When they spoke to you, they were with you. They weren't glancing at their phone or mentally crafting their next sentence.

They looked you in the eye - or if it was virtual, they made you feel like you were the only person in the world for that moment. You could feel their attention. And that presence? It made you feel seen. It said, *You matter. I'm here.* It didn't matter how profound or polished their words were - what mattered was that they showed up *fully* in the moment.

When my husband and I have something that's particularly important to talk about, we don't just speak in passing while folding laundry or watching TV. We sit next to each other. He turns toward me, and he listens - with no phone in his hand, no distractions. I can feel him *with* me. In that moment, I don't just feel heard - I feel respected, valued, and deeply loved. That's the power of presence. It's not about saying all the right things. It's about showing up with your whole self.

They were honest. Not in a harsh or performative way, but in a way that let you feel their heart. Even if they stumbled over their words, even if they didn't get it quite right, you knew they were being real. They didn't hide behind jargon or try to impress you. They simply told the truth as they understood it. You didn't have to wonder what they really meant. You could *feel* their sincerity, and that made it easy to trust them - even when the message was hard to hear.

I had an employee, Krystal, who modeled this kind of honesty better than most leaders I've known. She wasn't afraid to challenge me - but she always did it with intention and care. Sometimes she'd catch me off guard during a one-on-one and ask, "So how am I doing?" And I'd respond with a quick, distracted, "You're doing fine." She'd roll her eyes and say, "Okay, I need you to paint me a picture of that. What does *fine* look like? What am I doing that's fine? Or is it *great*? Help me understand what I'm doing well so I can do more of it." She was right - and I knew it. I wasn't being fully honest. Not because I didn't care, but because I was rushing. Avoiding depth. Playing it safe. The truth was, she wasn't just fine - she was *great*. But she was the one brave enough to invite the honesty I should have offered freely. And her honesty made me a better communicator, a better leader, and a more thoughtful human.

And they *followed through*. Their words matched their actions. If they said they'd do something, they did it. If they made a promise, they honored it. And if something changed, they circled back and let you know. Their communication wasn't just in what they said - it was in what they did *after* they said it. That kind of consistency builds safety. It reinforces trust. It shows people that your words aren't just noise - they *mean* something.

I once had a supervisor who fully embodied this. He had always supported my professional growth, and one day - after contemplating how to have a conversation that needed to be had with him - I walked into his office, closed the door, and asked, "Do you have a minute?" He looked up, clearly busy, and said, *"It better be fast - I've got to run to another meeting."* And I said, *"You need to hear this. I've been offered another job. The offer's sitting on my desk."* He paused. *"Have you signed it?"* I said no. He nodded and said, *"Okay. Give me until Tuesday. I'm confident I can work something out where you'll definitely want to stay."*

That was a Friday afternoon.

By Tuesday, not only had he followed through - he had pulled strings, advocated for me, and delivered exactly what he promised. A promotion. A pay increase. A new title. And most importantly, the respect, autonomy, and recognition I had been seeking. He didn't just say the right thing in the moment - he backed it up with action. That follow-through didn't just keep me in the organization - it deepened my trust and loyalty. Because I knew his words *meant something.*

That's what people really want. Not polish. Not perfection. But presence, honesty, and follow-through.

Not perfect grammar. Not witty remarks. Not impressing anyone with data points or inspirational quotes.

When we overthink communication, we tend to make it about *us* - how we're coming across, how we'll be perceived. But great communication is never about you. It's about the *relationship*. It's about the space between you and the person you're speaking to - and how you show up in that space. I like to say that between every challenge and solution is a space. We just need to be intentional about creating that space.

When we shift from performance to presence, everything changes.

Miscommunications become learning opportunities. Instead of rushing to defend ourselves or explain what we *meant* to say, we can lean into curiosity. We can ask, "How did that land for you?" or "What did you hear when I said that?" We stop assuming and start clarifying. And in doing so, we create space for repair instead of retreat. It's no longer about being right - it's about getting it right *together*.

Awkward moments become doorways to deeper understanding. We've all had those stumbles in conversation - the comment that didn't land, the long pause, the joke that missed the mark. But when we stop judging those moments as failures and start seeing them as part of being human, we open the door to honesty. We might say, "That came out wrong - can I try again?" or "I'm not sure how to say this, but I want to get it right." And just like that, vulnerability becomes connection.

Silence becomes a space for listening instead of a threat to fill. We stop scrambling to prove ourselves in every gap. We begin to trust that presence speaks louder than words. We become more comfortable with pausing, with letting others reflect, and with holding space for what's *not* being said. In that quiet, understanding grows. And often, the most meaningful connection happens in the spaces between our words.

And when you embrace the idea that what people really want from you is *you* - not a polished version, not a perfect communicator, but a *present*, caring, curious human - everything gets lighter. Easier. More real.

The goal isn't to master communication.

The goal is to *connect*.

STOP Overthinking It

Pause. Reflect. Apply.

What to Remember

- Perfect communication is a myth - and a barrier to real connection.
- People don't want polish. They want presence, honesty, and consistency.
- You don't need the perfect words. You just need to care enough to try.
- Overcorrecting, overthinking, and self-editing disconnect us from others and ourselves.
- Your humanness is what makes you trustworthy - not your flawlessness.

Self-Reflection

Take a few minutes to consider the following:

1. When have I overcorrected myself in a conversation - and why?
2. What's one recent moment where I held back instead of speaking up?
3. Who in my life models presence, honesty, or follow-through in communication? What impact does that have on me?
4. What am I afraid might happen if I say the "wrong" thing?
5. How would my relationships shift if I allowed myself to show up with more presence and less polish?

Try This Strategy

The Presence Check-In

Before your next important conversation, ask yourself:

Am I here, or in my head?

What's my intention - not just what I want to say, but how I want them to feel?

Can I allow myself to be imperfect in service of being real?

Then... speak. Even if it's messy. Even if your voice shakes. Even if you have to pause and say, "Let me try that again."

Presence over perfection - every time.

Conversation Starter

"What's something someone said to you that stuck—not because it was perfectly worded, but because it was real?"

This simple prompt opens the door for stories, insight, and emotional connection - and reminds everyone at the table of the power of authenticity.

Chapter 3

The New Belonging Crisis

Why people feel unseen in hyper-connected times - and how we can fix that.

Let's just start with the truth.

Most people don't feel like they belong.

They're not going to say it out loud - at least not right away.

But it shows up in quieter ways.

In the co-worker who turns their camera off and barely speaks during meetings.

In the friend who slowly stops reaching out.

In the employee who never shares an idea unless someone else says it first.

In the person who scrolls through social media, wondering why everyone else seems to have it all together.

It's this subtle ache.

Like you're always on the outside, even when you're technically "in."

And the worst part?

We're surrounded by more people, platforms, and conversations than ever before - yet we've never felt more disconnected.

That's not just a feeling. It's now considered a public health crisis.

According to the U.S. Surgeon General, loneliness and social disconnection have the same impact on our health as smoking up to 15 cigarettes a day [1].

Think about that.

In a world where we can FaceTime someone across the globe in seconds, people are *suffocating in silence.*

I remember the feeling of suffocating in silence.

And the truth is - it's not just a memory.

It still happens.

Even now.

I run a company that develops and delivers professional development training for organizations across the country. On paper, it sounds like I'm always "in the room," always confident, always leading. And in many ways, I am.

But every time I walk into a training (virtual or in-person) - especially on that first day - it feels a lot like the first day of school all over again.

People already know each other.

They've worked together, shared inside jokes, built trust.

And there I am. The outsider. Again.

At first, I feel the familiar pull - observe, adapt, blend.

But then… something shifts.

I start connecting ideas.

I ask questions that invite quieter folks into the conversation.

I share stories - funny, honest, human ones.

I encourage the over-sharers to bring others along, not just lead the room.

Slowly, the energy shifts. The group begins to breathe together.

And suddenly, the silence doesn't feel so suffocating - for me or for them.

We find belonging in the shared experience.

Some of the most beautiful moments happen when I'm training individuals from multiple organizations in the same room - where *everyone* walks in feeling like the outsider. And yet, by the end, they're laughing together. They're opening up. They're sharing stories about their work, their lives, their *humanness*.

Because belonging doesn't require history - it requires *presence*.

I felt it again recently, outside of work. I joined my local Rotary Club.

First meeting. New room. New faces. Everyone seemed to know where to sit. What to say. How it all worked.

I stood in the lobby, waiting for my sponsor to arrive, scanning the name tags and looking for a familiar face - any face.

And just like that, I was 13 years old again, holding a cafeteria tray, wondering where to sit.

It took everything in me not to turn around and leave.

And it's not like one day you say, *"I'm going to join Rotary,"* and suddenly you're in.

It's a process.

You attend a meeting. Then another.

You shake hands, smile, try to remember names.

You fill out an application.

The board votes to accept your membership.

And even after that... it still kind of feels like you're on the outside looking in.

You're *technically* a member, but you haven't quite found your footing yet.

You're included, but not fully integrated.

And that space in-between?

That's where the ache of "almost-belonging" lives.

My sponsor is like the cool kid in school - the one who knows everyone, who remembers details about everyone, who walks into the room with effortless charm. And there I am, clinging awkwardly to her orbit, trying not to make it obvious. She invites me to the parties. She introduces me to the people I "need to know." She creates the bridge.

But in the end?

It's up to *me* to walk across it.

I'm a natural introvert. I do fine one-on-one. I love meaningful conversation. But small talk in a crowded room of confident, accomplished people?

That's a deep breath, a pep talk in the car, and a prayer.

So I do what I've always done.

I watch.

I listen.

I study the room.

I start collecting little pieces of people - the way someone lights up when they talk about their grandkids, the person who always sneaks in two minutes before the meeting starts, the man who cracks dry jokes that only land with half the table.

I file it all away, because that's what I've always done. That's how I survive discomfort.

By observing first - then finding my way in.

And the more I talk to people, the more I realize - this is how a *lot* of us move through the world.

Watching.

Waiting.

Gathering information so we can figure out who we're supposed to be in the room.

We don't just do this in social clubs.

We do it in the workplace.

In friend groups.

In our neighborhoods.

Even in our own families.

We scan the environment, looking for signs.

Do I belong here?

Can I be myself here?

Is it safe to show up fully - or should I hold something back?

And if we don't get a clear answer, we retreat.

We smile politely.

We stick to the surface.

We keep our observations tucked in our back pocket, waiting for the moment when it feels safe enough to *exhale*.

The hard truth is that adults aren't immune to these feelings - we've just gotten better at hiding them.

And that hiding? That slow, subtle pulling back?

It chips away at our sense of connection over time.

We start to show up less, share less, trust less.

We convince ourselves that maybe we're just "different," or maybe we're just not that good at connecting.

But really, what we're experiencing isn't a personal failing.

It's the new belonging crisis.

The Quiet Cost of Disconnection

We're starved for spaces where we don't have to prove ourselves.

Where we're not sizing people up - or being sized up.

Where we can *be*, not just *perform*.

This isn't just about introverts or new members or sensitive souls.

This is about *humans*.

All of us.

Because according to the science, our brains are *wired* for belonging.

Dr. Matthew Lieberman found that our need to connect with others is as fundamental as our need for food and water [2].

Connection isn't just a "nice to have."

It's a biological necessity.

And when we don't feel it, everything else - our focus, our creativity, our physical health - starts to suffer.

Not because we're weak.

Because we're *wired* for each other.

One of the world's leading researchers on social neuroscience, Dr. Lieberman discovered something fascinating in his work: our brains interpret social pain - like rejection, exclusion, or loneliness - in the *same* way they process physical pain [2].

Let that sink in for a second.

When we feel left out or unseen, our brain doesn't just file it away as an emotional bummer - it processes that pain as if we've been physically hurt. This explains why disconnection can feel so intense, even when nothing "big" happened. It's not just in our heads. It's literally in our nervous system.

I think about a woman I once coached - let's call her Tanya. She was a brilliant team member, deeply creative, with a heart for mentoring others. But after a company merger, everything shifted. New leadership came in, teams were shuffled, and Tanya's role changed overnight. Her input wasn't sought like it used to be. She stopped getting invited to key meetings. The people she had mentored moved on to new roles, and no one filled the gap she left.

When we sat down to talk, she said something I'll never forget. "It's like I disappeared, but I'm still here. I come to work, I do what's expected, but no one really *sees* me anymore."

That's what social pain sounds like. And it's *real*.

It wasn't that she wanted constant praise or to be the center of attention - she just wanted to feel like she still mattered. That her voice still carried weight. That she still belonged in the place she had helped build.

This is what Lieberman's research helps us understand: connection isn't just a *nice feeling*. It's a *survival mechanism*. We are biologically wired to find belonging because, for most of human history, being excluded from the group could literally mean death. Our nervous system evolved to treat isolation as a threat because it *was* one.

And even now, in our modern lives with key cards and Zoom meetings and wellness programs, the threat of being emotionally left out still sets off alarms in our body.

So when someone feels invisible at work - or sits through a family dinner feeling like a ghost - it's not just uncomfortable. It's painful. It's damaging. And it's entirely human.

The Power of Being Seen

So if we know this pain is real - if we understand that people are walking around every day feeling unseen, unimportant, or quietly erased - then the next question has to be:

What do we do about it?

How do we create moments that send the opposite message?

Moments that say: *You matter. I see you. You belong here.*

Because if disconnection can happen in the smallest of moments - a meeting you weren't invited to, a smile that never reached your direction, a "How are you?" that felt more like a formality than a question - then reconnection can happen in small moments, too.

We fix the belonging crisis *one intentional moment at a time.*

It's not about grand gestures or perfectly orchestrated inclusion strategies. It's about presence. It's about noticing. It's about remembering that every person we interact with is carrying a story we can't fully see - and that story is begging to be acknowledged.

Sometimes, it's as simple as saying someone's name when they walk in the room.

Sometimes, it's circling back to a quieter voice in a meeting and saying, "Hey, what did you think?"

Sometimes, it's asking, "What's something you've been proud of lately?" instead of "What do you do?"

We can't fix the world all at once.

But we *can* help someone feel a little more seen today than they did yesterday.

That's how we start to fix what's broken.

We stop overthinking the perfect thing to say.

We start showing up with curiosity, consistency, and care.

We move from digital *contact* to human *connection.*

Real Recognition Changes Everything

I still remember one moment where I truly felt seen - and I didn't even realize how much I needed it until it happened.

At the time, I was a volunteer managing my organization's giving campaign for the United Way. It was a cause I cared about, and I poured my heart into it. I wasn't doing it for recognition - I just wanted to make a difference.

But the local United Way director saw something more in me.

She didn't just offer support - she *recognized* me. She invited me to train nonprofit agencies on how to craft and deliver their elevator pitches. She noticed my ability to encourage, to present, to connect with people - and she made space for me to use those gifts.

She didn't just thank me.

She *trusted* me.

She *included* me.

She later asked me to serve on the grant review committee, helping evaluate prospective recipients for United Way funding. I became a trusted part of a group that was making real decisions, doing meaningful work. And for one of the first times in my adult life, I didn't just feel helpful - I felt *valued*. Like I wasn't just participating, but I actually fit in.

That one leader's willingness to say, *"I see what you bring,"* changed how I saw myself.

It's been nearly a decade since that chapter of my life, and we still stay in touch. She continues to encourage me - to this day, she reaches out through social media to cheer on my work, to offer kind words, to remind me of what she saw in me back then.

And that's the thing about being seen.

It sticks with you.

It anchors you.

It reminds you of who you are - even on the days you forget.

We don't always realize the impact we have on people.

A kind word might feel small in the moment, but to someone who's been feeling invisible, it can mean everything.

We all carry the power to make someone feel seen, but too often, we hold back because we overthink it.

We assume they already know they're doing a good job.

We worry we'll sound awkward if we say something personal.

We convince ourselves we need to say it just right, so we wait.

And then we miss the moment.

But connection doesn't need a script.

It just needs intention.

What that United Way director did for me wasn't complicated. She noticed. She named what she saw. She extended trust and opportunity. And in doing so, she helped unlock something in me that I hadn't fully owned yet.

We can all do that.

You don't have to be someone's manager, mentor, or board chair to make them feel like they matter.

You just have to notice something real, and say it out loud.

"I see how you showed up in that meeting. That took courage."

"Your questions are always thoughtful. They help me think more clearly."

"I really admire the way you handled that situation. You have a gift."

It doesn't have to be big.

It just has to be honest.

Because in a world full of filtered images, half-listening, and performative praise, *real* recognition cuts through the noise.

The most beautiful part? When you see someone - *truly* see them - it often gives them permission to stop hiding.

When someone sees you - really sees you - it quiets the ache of disconnection.

It's like exhaling after holding your breath for too long.

It tells your nervous system: *You're safe now. You can let your guard down.*

That's not just poetic language - it's biology.

According to research from the Surgeon General's Advisory on Social Connection, even small moments of being acknowledged, like eye contact, a kind word, or a genuine check-in, help regulate our stress response, boost our mood, and increase our overall sense of well-being [1]. In short? Being seen calms the part of us that's been bracing for rejection.

I once trained a group of front-line healthcare workers who were burned out beyond belief. It was one of those sessions where the air in the room was heavy - tired faces, arms crossed, people waiting for the training to just *be over*.

But halfway through, I paused and said something simple:

> *"I want to acknowledge something I see in you. You keep showing up. Even on the hard days. And I know most people don't say thank you often enough - but I'm saying it now. You matter. What you do matters. And I see the effort you're making, even if no one else has said it lately."*

That moment changed the room.

A few people looked down. One woman quietly wiped a tear. The posture softened. The tension eased.

And what followed was the most open, human conversation we'd had all day.

All because someone said out loud what was true:

I see you. And you matter.

When we name someone's value, we remind them of it.

And when people feel seen, they stop shrinking. They start showing up.

So if you've been feeling unseen - if you've ever walked into a room and wondered whether anyone would notice if you slipped right back out - please hear me when I say this:

You are not invisible.

You are not too much.

You are not alone in this feeling.

You are worthy of being seen *exactly* as you are - no costume, no performance, no polish required.

And if no one has told you lately:

I see you.

I see the effort you're making.

I see the way you care deeply, even when you're exhausted.

I see how much you want to belong without having to bend yourself into someone else's shape.

You don't need to earn connection.

You just need to show up - real, human, and open-hearted.

And maybe, just maybe, that will help someone else feel safe enough to do the same.

That's how we begin to fix this crisis.

Not with perfection, but with presence.

Not by knowing exactly what to say, but by saying something real.

Let's make that our new goal - not to be impressive, but to be intentional.

Let's be the kind of people who help others feel *seen*.

STOP OVERTHINKING IT

PAUSE. REFLECT. APPLY.

What to Remember

- Feeling unseen isn't a personal flaw - it's a widespread, human experience in our hyper-connected world.
- Our brains are wired for connection, and when we feel invisible, it affects us emotionally *and* physically.
- Belonging isn't earned through performance. It grows through presence, honesty, and trust.
- You don't have to say something perfectly to make someone feel seen - you just have to mean it.
- Tiny moments - eye contact, acknowledgment, remembering a name - are powerful medicine for disconnection.
- Helping someone else feel seen often helps *you* reconnect with yourself, too.

Self-Reflection

1. Take a few minutes to explore these questions - whether through journaling, quiet thought, or conversation:
2. Where in my life do I feel most unseen or overlooked?
3. Who has helped me feel truly seen - and what did they do that made it meaningful?
4. When have I unintentionally made someone else feel invisible? How might I repair or shift that?
5. What might change if I began to notice and acknowledge others more intentionally?
6. What does *belonging* feel like to me - and where have I experienced it most?

Try This Strategy

The "I See You" Moment

Choose one person in your life - personal or professional - and take 60 seconds to reflect on something you genuinely appreciate about them. It could be their consistency, their kindness, their humor, or something they've done recently that mattered.

Then tell them.

Out loud. In writing. With a sticky note. In a text message. Doesn't matter how. Just say it.

"I see how hard you're working - thank you."

"You bring so much calm into our space."

"The way you encouraged that new team member really stood out to me."

Don't overthink it. Don't try to make it profound. Just make it *real*.

Conversation Starter

Use this question with a friend, teammate, or group to spark honest reflection:

"Can you think of a time when someone made you feel truly seen? What did they do - or not do - that made the difference?"

You might be surprised how healing it feels to revisit those moments - and how inspiring it is to pass them on.

PART II

The Heart of Connection

Chapter 4

Start with Curiosity

The antidote to assumption, judgment, and disconnection.

If there's one practice that has softened my relationships more than anything else - personally, professionally, even with myself - it's this: curiosity.

Genuine, open-hearted, *I-don't-have-it-all-figured-out* curiosity.

Because here's what I've learned the hard way:

We miss so many opportunities for connection because we think we already know.

We assume.

We label.

We jump to conclusions.

And we do it fast.

Sometimes we write an entire story in our heads before someone has even opened their mouth.

We decide someone's cold because they didn't say hi.

We assume someone doesn't like us because they didn't laugh at our joke.

We think the quiet team member doesn't care. The chatty one is too much. The boss is intimidating. The coworker is flaky. The client is rude.

But what if there's something we *don't* know?

What if the quiet person was up all night caring for a sick parent?

What if the "rude" client is terrified of being let down again?

What if the leader who seems distant is just trying to hold it all together?

Curiosity interrupts the stories we make up.

It widens the lens.

It replaces judgment with understanding.

And it opens a door to something deeper than politeness or assumption. It opens the door to real connection.

I used to think that to become an HR Director, I had to know *everything*. Every policy. Every law. Every process, from classification to compensation to labor negotiations. I thought leadership meant having all the answers at the ready, and saying them with confidence.

So I did what high-achievers do: I overprepared. I collected hands-on experience in multiple HR areas, took college coursework, and earned my Senior Professional in Human Resources (SPHR) certification. On paper, I was doing it all right.

But even then, I couldn't shake the feeling that I was missing something.

I was overthinking every move, every decision, every email, every interaction. I kept wondering, *Do I really know enough to lead? What if someone asks a question I don't have the answer to? What if I mess this up?*

Then one day, I was sitting across from an employee who came in with a concern. It was a complicated situation - personal, sensitive, and not something covered in any HR manual. I felt the familiar panic creeping in. *I should know how to handle this. I should already have a plan. I should say something wise and comforting.*

But instead of offering advice or defaulting to my usual "fix it" mode, I paused. I took a breath. And I asked one simple question:

"Can you tell me more about what you're experiencing?"

That moment changed everything.

They softened. They shared more. And I realized something that's shaped how I lead to this day:

I didn't need to have the right answer. I just needed to *care enough to ask the right question.*

That's what curiosity does - it takes the pressure off perfection and makes space for connection.

In fact, research shows that curiosity increases empathy and reduces stereotyping [3]. When we get genuinely curious about others - especially when they seem difficult, distant, or different - it literally shifts how we see them. Our brains begin to rewire assumptions and open up to understanding.

We stop putting people into boxes. We start seeing them as human.

Curiosity rewrites our stories - and that's where real connection takes root.

Curiosity Rewrites Our Stories

There have been people who assumed things about me - who labeled me based on a single interaction, a moment of confidence, a decision they didn't fully understand. And the hardest part wasn't that they misunderstood me. It was that they never asked a single question.

They never asked where I came from.

What shaped me.

What mattered to me.

What I was carrying.

They never asked what it felt like to walk into a room as the only woman in leadership.

Or what it took for me to hold it together while navigating a personal storm.

They never asked who I really was behind the title, the degrees, the smile.

And when people don't ask, when they assume instead, they stop seeing you as a whole person. You become a role. A résumé. A reaction they misread. A character they filled in with their own unfinished story.

That's what assumption does.

It reduces people.

It turns living, complex humans into caricatures.

And the sad part? It's often unintentional.

Most of the time, we're not trying to be dismissive or cold - we're just *busy*. We're rushing. We're focused on our task list. We default to shortcuts. But the brain's desire for efficiency can come at the cost of empathy.

Dr. Matthew Lieberman explains this in his research on social cognition, our brain is wired to *automatically* make quick judgments about people to help us navigate the social world [2]. But unless we pause to question those automatic thoughts, unless we *get curious*, we end up relating to people based on surface-level data, not real connection.

We stop short of understanding.

And the result is more of what we're already seeing: isolation, disconnection, mistrust.

But there's good news.

Curiosity is a skill we can strengthen.

And sometimes, it only takes one question to change everything.

So how do we actually practice curiosity? Especially when we've been conditioned to lead with conclusions instead of questions?

It starts with something small but powerful: the willingness to pause.

Pausing gives us just enough space to interrupt the default assumptions our brain wants to make. It gives us room to notice, to ask, to listen. And this isn't just feel-good advice; it's supported by research. According to a 2021 study published in the journal *Social Psychological and Personality Science*, people who ask more questions, especially follow-up questions, are perceived as more responsive, more likable, and more interested in others [4].

In other words, asking questions isn't just a soft skill, it's a social superpower.

But here's the catch: curiosity takes courage.

It asks us to admit we don't know everything.

To lean into the discomfort of uncertainty.

To release our grip on being right, and open ourselves to being surprised.

That can feel vulnerable, especially in workplaces where people fear being judged for asking "dumb" questions or not having it all figured out. But vulnerability is the price of connection, and curiosity is its doorway.

As Brené Brown reminds us, vulnerability isn't weakness—it's courage in its rawest form. It's the willingness to show up without a guarantee of how it'll be received. And curiosity is one of the ways we practice that courage. It's how we say, *I don't know everything, but I care enough to understand.*

Have you ever had a burning question during a meeting, but no one else was speaking up, so you held it?

You sat there, heart racing, wondering *Am I the only one confused?*

You scanned the room, hoping someone else would ask it. But everyone stayed quiet, brows furrowed, eyes flicking toward the clock and the others in the room. And you convinced yourself it wasn't worth asking.

Better to stay silent than risk looking stupid.

Better to pretend you get it than admit you don't.

Better to *look smart* than feel seen.

I remember one time, early in my leadership journey, I was in a cross-department meeting where we were discussing a huge organizational change, something that would affect hundreds of employees. The language being used was all jargon, full of terms I didn't fully understand. I had a thousand questions. But no one was asking any. People were nodding, taking notes, nodding again.

So I stayed quiet.

And the meeting ended with confusion hanging in the air, unspoken but palpable. Later that day, one of my colleagues stopped by my office and said, "I had no idea what they were talking about. Did you?" I laughed and admitted, "Not really." She sighed, "I wish someone had asked a question. I almost did, but…"

We both almost did.

That moment stuck with me.

Because sometimes, asking the question isn't just about *you*.

It's about the signal it sends to others.

Courage is Contagious

It says: It's okay to not know. It's okay to ask. It's okay to care enough to seek clarity.

And more often than not, your courage becomes someone else's permission.

We can start small.

Curiosity doesn't require a personality overhaul or a new job title. It doesn't require extroversion or endless free time. It just asks us to be a little more intentional.

Ask one question.

Follow up when someone gives a half-answer.

Resist the urge to assume you already know the whole story.

Instead of jumping to conclusions, pause and wonder:

> *What else might be true here?*

Instead of thinking, *That was a weird reaction,* try:

> *I wonder what might be going on beneath the surface.*

These micro-moments of curiosity can change the tone of a meeting, shift a relationship, even soften conflict. And when practiced consistently, they build something powerful: *psychological safety.*

Teams thrive in environments where questions are welcome, not penalized. Where people don't have to posture or pretend. Research from Google's Project Aristotle found that psychological safety, more than intelligence, experience, or talent, was the number one predictor of team success [5]. And what fosters that safety?

Curiosity.

Listening.

Willingness to not have it all figured out.

When leaders and teammates ask real questions, they model humility and openness. They show that no one's expected to be perfect. And that creates space for people to share honestly, offer ideas, and admit when they need support.

Curiosity creates space.

Judgment shrinks it.

And in a world where people already feel unseen and unsure, space is one of the greatest gifts you can give.

I've also overthought things in my personal life that curiosity could've saved.

There was a time, not too long ago, when I completely misread my husband's silence. We'd both had long days. I was buzzing with things I wanted to share, but he was quiet, withdrawn. I felt the shift, that space between us, and my mind went to work:

Did I say something wrong?

Is he upset with me?

Why is he being so distant?

I didn't ask. I stewed. I got snippy. I folded laundry with more aggression than necessary.

Finally, he asked, "Are you okay?"

And I answered with that classic deflection: "Ya. Why?" My default answer, which, by the way, he always knows that something is wrong. The question was rhetorical.

Turns out… he was just tired.

Completely worn out.

He wasn't mad. He wasn't disengaged. He wasn't thinking anything I imagined.

He just needed a moment to recharge before engaging.

And all I needed to do was ask.

One gentle question could have saved hours of inner spiraling.

One moment of *real* curiosity could've prevented the weird tension that neither of us deserved.

But instead of getting curious, I got in my head.

I let the silence fill with stories instead of filling it with connection.

This happens more than we realize.

We don't just overthink what *we* should say, we overthink what others *mean*, and then react to the version we made up instead of the reality they're living. Curiosity can interrupt that. It can help us trade assumptions for empathy, and inner narratives for real connection.

And the best part? You don't have to have the perfect question.

You just have to *want to understand more than you want to be right*.

Another unexpected gift of curiosity?

It deepens intimacy.

Not the surface-level kind that comes from "liking" someone's post or nodding through a conversation, but the kind that makes people feel truly known.

We all want to feel chosen - not just accepted, but *understood*.

And curiosity is how we say: *I want to know you, not just the version of you I see on the surface.*

Some of the closest connections in my life didn't start because someone wowed me with their story. They started when someone asked me something *real* - and listened to the answer.

"What lights you up right now?"

"What do you miss most about who you used to be?"

"What's something you wish people knew about you - but never ask?"

These kinds of questions? They crack people open in the best way.

They invite more than a yes/no response.

They say: *I want to go deeper. I'm not afraid of your truth.*

Curiosity isn't just about collecting information - it's about offering attention.

And in a world where people feel like they're always performing, attention is love.

In long-term relationships, curiosity keeps things alive. It's what turns autopilot into presence. It's what helps you keep discovering your partner, even after years. Because people aren't fixed. We change. We grow. We unravel and rebuild.

When we stop being curious, we stop being close.

But when we *stay* curious - when we keep asking, keep listening, keep being interested in the small, daily evolutions of someone's life - we build something strong. Something lasting.

We don't fall out of connection all at once. We drift.

Curiosity is what pulls us back in.

Curiosity isn't just about other people.

It's also one of the most healing things you can offer *yourself*.

When I first started untangling my own overthinking, I realized something: I wasn't just hard on other people, I was relentless with myself.

Any time I made a mistake, missed a text, forgot a birthday, said something awkward, I didn't respond with curiosity. I responded with shame. I'd spiral into *Why did I say that? What's wrong with me? When will I learn?* I'd launch a mental investigation, but it wasn't one rooted in kindness. It was interrogation disguised as reflection.

And honestly? It didn't help me grow. It just made me smaller. Because that's what judgement does. It keeps us in a shrunken space. A space where what we perceive as a flaw or a weakness is amplified and truth is muted.

It's loud and obnoxious and it keeps us from connecting to the truth.

But the moment I started asking softer questions, something shifted.

"Why did that moment hit so hard?"

"What do I need right now?"

"Where is this coming from, and what part of me is trying to protect me?"

These aren't judgmental questions. They're curious ones.

They help me meet myself, not just fix myself.

They help me move through hard moments with understanding instead of shame.

And you know what? That gentleness changes how I show up for others, too.

The more compassion I give myself, the less I expect others to read my mind, validate my worth, or guess how I'm feeling. I stop demanding perfection from everyone around me because I've stopped demanding it from myself.

That's the kind of curiosity that creates real freedom.

So if you're in a season of doubt, disconnection, or just plain tired of second-guessing everything - start here:

Ask yourself what you need.

Ask yourself what you're afraid of.

Ask yourself how you're really doing.

And when the answer comes? Don't rush to fix it.

Just *listen*.

That's where reconnection begins.

So if you've been overthinking what to say, how to show up, or whether you're getting it "right" - take a breath.

You don't have to know all the answers.

You don't have to lead with the perfect insight or the most polished response.

You just have to be *willing to wonder*.

Because curiosity is a bridge.

It connects us when the words don't come easily.

It softens judgment, quiets fear, and brings us back into relationship - with others, and with ourselves.

You don't have to come up with something brilliant.

You just have to ask a better question.

One rooted in kindness, in openness, in *I care enough to ask*.

And when you do that, you create space for something deeper than approval or agreement:

You create space for connection.

Stay curious.

Even when you're tired.

You don't have to have it all figured out to be someone else's bright spot.

Even when it feels awkward.

Even when it's easier to retreat.

Because curiosity isn't just a communication skill.

It's a way of saying: *I see you. I care enough to stay with you here.* And that's where connection begins.

It's an act of love.

STOP OVERTHINKING IT

Pause. Reflect. Apply.

What to Remember

- Curiosity interrupts judgment. It helps us see people - and ourselves - more clearly.
- You don't need the perfect question. You just need a sincere desire to understand.
- Assumptions shrink relationships. Curiosity expands them.
- You can't connect deeply if you're only engaging with the version of people you've invented in your head.
- Small moments of curiosity - "Tell me more," "What's going on for you?" - can completely shift a conversation.
- Curiosity builds empathy, trust, intimacy, and psychological safety - in every kind of relationship, including the one with yourself.

Self-Reflection

Set a timer for 10 minutes, grab a pen or open your notes app, and explore:

1. When was the last time I made an assumption that turned out to be wrong?
2. Where in my life do I tend to overthink instead of ask?
3. What relationships in my life could benefit from more curiosity?
4. What's a part of *myself* I've been judging lately - could I get curious instead?
5. What might open up if I replaced "What's wrong with me?" with "What might I need right now?"

Try This Strategy

The "Tell Me More" Rule

This week, in at least one conversation, try replacing a reaction or opinion with a question. Specifically, this one:

"Tell me more about that."

It works in almost any situation - at work, with family, with your partner, or even with a stranger.

You don't have to fix, respond, or agree.

Just ask. Then listen.

Bonus points if you use it with yourself, too.

"Tell me more..."

Why am I feeling this way? What's underneath it? What's trying to get my attention?

Simple. Gentle. Powerful.

Conversation Starter

Use this with a friend, team, or loved one:

"What's something people often assume about you that isn't true?"

This one opens the door for honesty, vulnerability, and a deeper understanding of the person behind the surface. You'll probably be surprised by what you learn - and how much closer you feel afterward.

Chapter 5

Real > Right

Authenticity builds more trust than saying the "right" thing.

There was a time in my life when I thought the fastest way to connection was to always say the "right" thing. The polished thing. The thing that made me look confident, wise, put together. It was never about lying - it was about filtering. Softening. Reading the room and delivering what I thought would land.

And in some ways, it worked. People respected me. They listened. I was often praised for being articulate, for knowing how to "say things well."

But here's what they didn't know: behind the scenes, I was exhausted. I was overthinking every sentence. Replaying every conversation. Wondering if I'd said too much, or not enough. Wondering if my "right" words had actually reached anyone at all.

Because there's a difference between being heard and being felt.

And I was missing that second part.

I started to notice this gap when I began leading more teams, coaching more leaders, and sitting in conversations where tension was high and trust was low. I'd watch people say all the "right" things - "I understand," "That makes sense," "We'll take that into consideration" - but the energy in the room would stay cold. No movement. No shift.

And then someone would speak up and say something clumsy, but real:

> *"This is hard for me to say, but I'm struggling with this decision."*
>
> *"I might not say this perfectly, but I want to be honest."*
>
> *"I'm nervous to share this, but I think it needs to be said."*

Suddenly, the temperature changed. Shoulders dropped. People nodded. You could feel the room breathe again.

It wasn't about getting it "right." It was about being *real*.

In fact, research confirms this. A 2020 Harvard Business Review article highlighted that **authenticity is one of the top three traits people look for in their leaders** - even more than competence or charisma [6]. Why? Because authenticity signals safety. When someone is real with us, we don't feel like we're being manipulated or managed. We feel like we're being met.

Authenticity builds trust, not because it's flawless - but because it's *human*.

Real Beats Perfect

I remember once, during a high-stakes meeting with a client, I totally blanked. I was supposed to walk them through a new leadership framework, and suddenly - poof - my brain just... stopped cooperating. I could feel the panic bubbling up, the inner critic shouting, "You're blowing it. You're supposed to be the expert!"

But instead of powering through with jargon or faking my way through the rest of the presentation, I paused. I took a breath and said:

"I'm going to be really honest. I just lost my train of thought. Give me a second."

And you know what happened?

The client smiled and said, "Thank you. That actually makes me feel better. I've been so nervous about having to present next week."

We laughed. I found my footing. And the rest of the session was one of the most engaging, collaborative conversations we had all year.

Because I didn't posture. I didn't pretend. I let them see me, and in doing that, they let their guard down too.

I've seen this play out so many times during interviews.

When I was hiring, especially for roles people *really* wanted, candidates would often walk in with rehearsed answers. They'd sit up straight, smile too wide, and tell me what they thought I wanted to hear.

They weren't trying to be deceptive. They were trying to be chosen.

But in that effort, they often lost the most important thing they had to offer: themselves.

I could feel it when it happened - that slight shift when someone stopped being present and started performing. The overly polished answers. The safe stories. The buzzwords and phrases they picked up from career blogs or mock interviews. It all made sense... but it didn't *land*.

So I started getting more intentional. I'd slow down the conversation. I'd ask questions that weren't on the standard list. I'd let the silence stretch a little, just long enough to signal, *You don't have to perform here. You can just be you.*

And almost every time, there'd be this moment - a breath, a laugh, a shift in posture - and they'd drop the script.

That's when the real conversation would begin.

They'd tell me about the project they were proud of, not because it was perfect, but because it was hard. They'd share a failure and what they learned. They'd let me see who they were - not just what they'd accomplished. And that's where trust began.

Because here's the truth I wish more people knew: you're not hired for being perfect.

You're hired because someone believes you're the right person to grow with the team. To bring something real to the table. To adapt, contribute, and keep learning.

And we can't see *any* of that if you're just giving us what you think we want to hear.

Beyond the Polished Parts

I learned early in life not to let too many people in. When you change schools thirty-three times, you become skilled at surface-level connections - quick friendships, just enough openness to get by, but not enough to risk getting hurt. It was survival. But over time, that self-protection became habit. Even as an adult, I kept parts of myself tucked away, out of reach. I thought being strong meant keeping it together. I thought being respected meant keeping things private. And I thought being loved meant not being a burden.

But I've learned something else: the people who really love you want *all* of you - not just the polished parts.

That lesson hit hardest when I finally came clean with people close to me about the truth I had been hiding. I told them I was in a domestic violence relationship. I told them I was scared. That I didn't know how I let it get this far. That I didn't know what to do. For so long, I'd kept it to myself, convinced I needed to be the strong one. After all, I was the one people looked up to - the achiever, the helper, the one with all the answers.

But that wasn't the full story. Not even close.

And when I finally let down the mask and spoke the truth - not perfectly, not with a plan, but with honesty - something shifted. People didn't run. They leaned in. They reached out. They offered support I hadn't even known how to ask for. Because before that moment, they hadn't seen the whole picture. They saw what I let them see. And the version I'd shown wasn't someone they thought needed help.

That experience taught me that vulnerability isn't weakness - it's clarity. It lets people love the real you. It gives them permission to show up for you. And it builds trust in a way that performance never can.

Because when you let people see your fear, your heartbreak, your uncertainty - and they choose to stay? That's connection.

That's when you know it's real.

That kind of raw honesty - telling someone what's *really* going on - can feel like a massive leap. And sometimes, it is. But authenticity doesn't always require a grand reveal or a heavy conversation. Most of the time, it shows up in much smaller moments.

It looks like saying, *"I'm not totally sure what you mean. Can you walk me through that again?"*

It sounds like replying to a text with, *"I don't have the right words right now, but I'm thinking of you."*

It shows up in meetings when someone says, *"I don't have a fully baked idea yet, but here's what I'm thinking…"*

Or in a message to a client: *"I'm double-checking this for you because I want to make sure it's right."*

These small, honest signals build trust. They tell people: I care more about being real with you than about being impressive. And that's a rare gift - especially in a world where so many people are taught to lead with polish over presence.

When I would interview job candidates, I could always tell who had been trained to say what they thought I wanted to hear. Their answers were rehearsed. Safe. Bland. I'd ask a question, and I could almost see the gears turning: *What's the "right" response? What will make me sound good?* But the problem was, I didn't want a perfect answer - I wanted a human one.

So I'd slow things down. I'd share a little about my own imperfect path, drop the professional pretense, and create space for them to relax. Because once people feel safe, the real person starts to show up. And that's when the conversation actually begins. That's when you learn who they are - not just what they've memorized.

And that's not just true in interviews.

It's true in our friendships.

In our family group texts.

In hallway check-ins at work.

In every corner of our lives.

Authenticity isn't just "being yourself." It's trusting that *being yourself is enough*. It's choosing to show up, even if your voice shakes, even if your words aren't perfect, even if it feels like a risk. Because the right people don't need you to perform. They just need you to be real.

Authenticity doesn't just make you *likable* - it makes you *trustable*.

There's a reason why we gravitate toward people who aren't trying to perform. They're steady. Safe. You know where you stand with them. Even if you don't always agree, you know what they say is real. And in a world where so many conversations feel like a script, that kind of honesty is magnetic.

When I finally came clean about the domestic violence I was experiencing, it wasn't just about asking for help. It was about giving myself permission to stop pretending. To stop managing everyone else's perception of me. And when I did that - when I shared my truth instead of maintaining the shiny version of my life - something powerful happened: people leaned in.

Not with pity. Not with advice.

With presence.

With care.

With respect.

Because the moment I stopped hiding, I became more *relatable*. And suddenly, the people around me felt safer to share their truth too. It wasn't just me being vulnerable - it was an invitation. A ripple effect.

That's the thing about authenticity - it creates a kind of sacred permission.

When you let someone see the real you, you give them a soft place to land. You tell them, *You don't have to pretend here.*

That's how trust is built.

That's how belonging takes root.

Not in the highlight reels. Not in the perfect delivery. But in the real, honest, sometimes messy middle.

Think about the people you trust most. I'm willing to bet it's not because they always say the perfect thing. It's because they're consistent. They're human. They're honest about their highs and humble about their lows.

You don't have to bare your soul to every person you meet. But if you want deeper connection, you *do* have to stop armoring up.

You can't build intimacy from behind a mask.

And the tricky part? Sometimes, we don't even know we're wearing one.

We've worn the "I'm fine" mask for so long it starts to feel like our actual face. We've rehearsed the polished answer so many times that we forget what we actually believe. And we wonder why our relationships feel… distant. Hollow. A little off.

But when you finally speak from your truth - even if it's messy, even if it's unsure - you'll feel the difference. You'll notice the softening. You'll hear it in their voice, see it in their eyes. The connection changes. Deepens. Because *you* changed.

There's a certain kind of loneliness that comes from being misunderstood - not because people got you wrong, but because you never showed them the real version of you in the first place.

I know that kind of loneliness.

I lived it.

For much of my adult career, I felt like I had to play a part. I pretended to be an extrovert. I turned the volume up on my personality to match the energy I thought people expected from a leader. I wore the nicest clothes. Drove the nicest car. Walked into rooms trying to radiate confidence - even when inside, I felt like an imposter trying to hold it all together.

And here's the thing: it worked. Sort of.

People noticed. I got promoted. I was invited to the table. But I was also misunderstood. Labeled. Misread. People saw "over-the-top" when really, I was trying not to disappear. They saw a woman who had it all together - when the truth was, I was exhausted from holding it all up.

And for a long time, I blamed them for not seeing me clearly.

But the hardest truth I had to face was this: I never gave them the chance.

I didn't know how to articulate who I really was. I was so focused on being who I thought I *needed* to be to belong, to be taken seriously, to be admired - that I never asked what it would look like to just *be* me.

That's the trap of overthinking authenticity: you start to believe there's a *right* way to be real.

There isn't.

There's just you.

And once I began the uncomfortable, messy process of shedding those old roles - the "perfect professional," the "always-on" extrovert, the "unshakeable" leader - I started to feel something I hadn't felt in a long time: *known*.

Not just seen. Not just respected. But *known* - for who I was, not who I performed to be.

But let me be honest - it didn't happen overnight.

And it wasn't always well received.

When you shift how you show up, people who were used to the polished version of you might not know what to do with the raw one. Some people will lean in. Others might pull away. And that can feel like rejection - but it's actually clarity.

Because the people who stay?

They're the ones who love *you*. Not the persona. Not the projection. Just you.

And you? You get to stop performing. You get to breathe.

The shift didn't happen in a single, bold moment. It happened in small, quiet decisions.

The first time I said, *"I'm not okay"* when someone asked how I was doing.

The first time I shared that I was afraid.

The first time I admitted that I didn't know what to do next - and let someone else hold space for me instead of powering through on my own.

And you know what happened?

I didn't fall apart.

I didn't lose respect.

I didn't get laughed out of the room.

I got *closer* to people.

Because it turns out, letting people see your truth is what invites *their* truth to the surface too. It gives them permission to be honest, to exhale, to show up without the mask.

As Brené Brown reminds us, clarity is kindness. When we're real with others, we aren't burdening them - we're giving them something they can actually respond to with love, support, and understanding [7].

Vulnerability might feel risky - but it's also the birthplace of the kinds of relationships we're all craving: honest, supportive, safe, and real.

The more I opened up, the more those relationships deepened.

And the less I needed to prove myself.

But let's be real - authenticity doesn't always guarantee understanding.

There have still been times - *plenty* of them - when I've shown up fully, honestly, vulnerably… and someone didn't get it. They misunderstood my intent. They questioned my motives. They misread my tone. They responded to me based on an old version of who they thought I was, or projected their own stuff onto my words.

And those moments still sting.

It's tempting to shrink back after that. To think, *See? This is why I don't open up. This is why I stick to the script.*

But here's what I've learned: their misunderstanding doesn't make your truth any less valid.

Being misunderstood doesn't mean you did something wrong.

It means you took a risk.

It means you were brave enough to show up as yourself - and that's always a win, even if it doesn't land the way you hoped.

The real work isn't getting everyone to understand you.

The real work is continuing to understand *yourself*—and standing in that truth with kindness and clarity.

Because when you know who you are, and you're no longer trying to perform, defend, or explain yourself into belonging, something shifts inside you. There's peace. There's power. There's *freedom.*

You stop editing your personality to match the room.

You stop dimming your light to make other people comfortable.

You stop performing for applause - and start connecting for real.

So if you're in that space right now - struggling to be understood, tempted to go back to the polished version of yourself - take this as your reminder:

You don't need to be everyone's cup of tea.

You just need to be your own damn self.

The right people will get it.

And the ones who don't? That's not your burden to carry.

Keep showing up. Keep being real.

Even when it's awkward. Even when it's messy. Even when you're misunderstood.

Because connection isn't about being perfect.

It's about being *honest*.

STOP Overthinking It

Pause. Reflect. Apply.

What to Remember

- Saying the "right" thing doesn't build trust - being *real* does.
- People connect with your truth, not your polish.
- Authenticity invites clarity, connection, and courage - even if it's misunderstood sometimes.
- Vulnerability isn't weakness. It's how trust begins.
- You don't have to have it all together to be respected. You just have to be *you*.

Self-Reflection

Take a moment and ask yourself:

1. When was the last time I said what I thought someone wanted to hear instead of what I really felt?
2. What part of me have I been over-editing to fit in or be liked?
3. Who in my life sees the real me—and how does that feel?
4. Where am I still holding back out of fear of being misunderstood?
5. What might change if I gave myself permission to be 5% more honest in my relationships?

Try This Strategy

The Real Response Rule

Next time you catch yourself reaching for the polished answer or saying what you *think* you're supposed to say, pause.

Ask yourself:

What's the truer version of this response?

Then say that.

Even if it's softer. Even if it's unfinished. Even if it starts with, *"This might not come out right, but…"*

Start building trust by showing up as someone others can trust to be real.

Conversation Starter

Try this in your next real-life check-in - with a friend, a teammate, a partner, or even your reflection:

"What's something you wish people understood about you, but you rarely get a chance to say?"

This one's a door-opener. Be ready to really listen, and maybe even share your own truth, too.

Chapter 6

The Power of Being Seen

Recognition, validation, and everyday micro-moments that build trust.

There's a moment that still sits in my chest like it just happened yesterday. I was volunteering to lead our organization's United Way campaign - pouring in hours on top of my regular job, rallying people, organizing events, and doing it with heart. I wasn't looking for recognition; I just cared about the mission. But then something unexpected happened. The local United Way director of events and corporate engagement, Gail, saw what I was doing. I mean really *saw* it. She reached out - not just to thank me, but to invite me to train nonprofit leaders in our region on how to deliver effective elevator pitches. She said, *"You have a gift. You make people care. You see people. And that's what our grantees need."* She didn't just acknowledge my effort - she validated my impact.

That invitation led to a seat on their grant review committee and, later, a lasting professional relationship. We still stay in touch through social media, and every once in a while, she'll pop in with a message of encouragement. She saw something in me I hadn't fully owned yet. And in doing that, she helped me see it too.

That's the power of being seen.

According to the U.S. Surgeon General's Advisory on Social Connection (2023), a lack of meaningful social interaction is now considered a public health threat—with risks comparable to smoking fifteen cigarettes a day [1]. In other words: being unseen isn't just emotionally painful. It's physically harmful. Human beings are wired to connect. And that connection starts with something incredibly simple, but often overlooked - acknowledgment.

Dr. Brene Brown says, *"We are hardwired for connection, but the key is that, in any given moment of it, it has to be real"* [8]. Recognition that's performative doesn't feed us. Neither does blanket praise or generic thank-you's. What we crave is specific, personal, human recognition. We want someone to witness the truth of who we are - not just what we do.

And yet, so many of us go through our days feeling invisible.

At work, it can look like being left off the email. Not being asked for input. Giving our all and getting a "thanks" that barely lands. In relationships, it might feel like our emotional labor goes unnoticed. That no one sees how much we're carrying behind the scenes. That no one hears the quiet ways we show up.

But here's the truth: we all want to be seen. Not for show. Not for ego. But to know that our presence matters.

The psychological impact of being recognized is backed by research. Studies have shown that something as small as a personalized thank-you or calling someone by name can activate the brain's reward system [2]. Even brief, authentic acknowledgment can boost performance, increase belonging, and deepen trust within teams and relationships. It's not just feel-good fluff - it's neuroscience.

One of the most powerful frameworks to emerge in the last decade is Amy Edmondson's concept of *psychological safety* - the shared belief that a team is safe for interpersonal risk-taking. Being seen is one of its pillars.

When people feel invisible, they retreat. When they feel recognized, they contribute. Because they know they matter [9].

But here's where it gets real - *being seen isn't just about being praised.* Sometimes, it's about being understood.

It's when someone notices you're off and asks, *"Hey, are you okay?"*

It's when a friend remembers the anniversary of your loss and reaches out.

It's when your partner notices the way your shoulders slump at the end of the day and says, *"Come sit with me. You don't have to do this alone."* My husband, Steve, by the way, is great at this!

These small, quiet moments? They're everything. Dr. John Gottman calls them "bids for connection" - and whether we turn toward or away from them defines the health of our relationships [10].

So often, we get caught up in the big stuff: promotions, achievements, milestones. But real connection is built in the micro-moments. The glance. The gesture. The extra pause before we move on.

I've seen this in teams again and again - leaders who think their role is to drive outcomes forget that seeing people is the outcome. When employees are recognized for their unique strengths, their voice, their effort - not just their productivity - they don't just perform better. They stay. They care. They believe.

And it's not just the boss's job. We can all be "noticers."

We can say, *"I saw how you handled that client call. You stayed calm under pressure. That mattered."*

Or *"You've been showing up even when it's hard. I just want you to know - I notice."*

Or *"Your energy always lifts this space, and I'm grateful for you."*

These aren't dramatic declarations. They're real, grounded moments of human-to-human recognition. And they change the game.

But let's not forget this truth: being seen by others is important. But learning to *see ourselves*? That's transformational.

Because until we believe we are worthy of being seen - flawed, messy, human and all - we'll keep overthinking, overworking, and overcompensating to earn what was always ours to begin with: belonging.

That's the kind of truth that doesn't need a clever quote or perfect delivery. It just needs you to stop long enough to ask:

What would change if I really let myself be seen?

By others.

By myself.

And what would change if I became someone who really saw others, too?

Let's explore that.

When You're Forced to Be Seen

There's a quiet kind of grief that comes from not being seen - not because people intentionally ignore you, but because they assume they already know who you are. It's the grief of invisibility. The ache of being misunderstood.

For much of my adult life, I lived behind a carefully managed image. I wore the professional mask well. I was the achiever. The one who showed up, who kept it together, who said the "right" things and always looked polished. I led teams, mentored others, organized community events, ran giving campaigns. I was the person people leaned on. The one who helped everyone else.

But behind closed doors, I was living a nightmare.

My ex-husband was a police officer. And one night, he threatened to shoot me - along with my two daughters and my grandkids, who were in the house at the time.

That night, I made the decision that would change everything.

We ran. I called 911. And what followed wasn't immediate relief. It was the beginning of an entirely different kind of storm.

Suddenly, I had no choice but to tell the truth. To my daughters. To my boss. To my mother. To the people I had worked so hard to protect from seeing this part of my life. Some of them had sensed something. Most didn't know the extent of what I'd been hiding. But now, the mask was off. And the secret I had carried for so long could no longer stay hidden.

What I thought might bring shame… brought healing.

People showed up. My family, my colleagues, my boss - they rallied. They helped me find my footing, supported me as I created a new home, held space for my grief and fear and anger. And while I didn't choose to drop the mask in some brave, calculated moment of vulnerability - I *was* forced to take it off - I'm so grateful that I did.

Because that's when I truly started to feel seen.

Not for my strength or my accomplishments or the image I curated - but for the woman underneath it all. The woman who was scared. Exhausted. Trying to rebuild. The woman who had spent so long hiding her truth, and who finally, out of necessity, had to let it be known.

And once I did? I experienced something I'll never forget:

I was still loved.

I was still respected.

I was still whole.

Not because I was flawless - but because I was finally real.

That's what being seen can do. It doesn't just heal the heartache of invisibility - it repairs the broken belief that we only deserve connection when we're at our best. It reminds us that love, support, and belonging are still available - even when we're messy, raw, and just trying to survive.

That experience changed me.

It changed how I lead, how I listen, and how I show up - because I know what it feels like to walk into a room carrying something heavy and invisible. I know what it feels like to be surrounded by people and still feel alone. And I know how much one genuine moment of being seen can change everything.

When someone looks past your title, your resume, your performance, and sees the person.

Not the helper. Not the achiever. Not the fixer. You.

We all have the ability to give that to each other.

But too often, we move too fast to notice what someone might be carrying. We ask, "How are you?" as a greeting, not a question. We praise performance but miss the person. We celebrate strength without acknowledging the quiet courage it takes just to show up some days.

Being seen isn't about grand gestures.

It's about the micro-moments.

Noticing when someone's voice changes during a meeting and checking in after. Remembering that a colleague mentioned their child had surgery and following up a week later. Offering space when someone seems off - without needing them to explain. These moments don't take much. But they matter more than we know.

Because as humans, we're wired to want recognition - not in the egoic sense, but in the primal, social sense. According to the U.S. Surgeon General's 2023 Advisory on the Healing Effects of Social Connection, a lack of meaningful social interaction increases the risk of premature death by more than 60% [1]. Being seen isn't just "nice to have" - it's *necessary*.

The research backs it up.

Dr. Matthew Lieberman's work in social neuroscience shows that our need to connect is as fundamental as our need for food and water [2]. When we feel excluded or ignored, the same parts of the brain that process physical pain light up. That's why being overlooked doesn't just sting - it *hurts*.

But the good news?

We can each be part of the healing.

We can be the ones who slow down long enough to really look at someone.

To really *see* them.

To say, *"I notice you. I appreciate you. You matter."*

And when we do that, something shifts - not just in them, but in us.

Because seeing someone else with empathy, with attention, with curiosity - it softens us. It reminds us what matters. It brings us back to our shared humanity.

And that's what connection is all about.

It's not about having all the right words or fixing someone's pain.

It's about showing up with your eyes, your ears, and your heart open - and letting someone know they're not invisible.

That you see them.

And that's enough.

How We Practice Seeing Each Other

You don't need a Ph.D. in psychology or hours of training to help someone feel seen.

You just need intention.

It starts with choosing to notice. In a world that rewards speed, productivity, and polish, seeing someone requires us to slow down long enough to actually *look*.

And it's not just about noticing what's *wrong*. It's also noticing what's *right*. Too often we're quick to give feedback when there's a problem - but slow to recognize the everyday effort, the quiet wins, the resilience that people show without fanfare.

Think about the colleague who always catches the details others miss. The friend who checks in on everyone but rarely gets checked in on. The parent quietly holding it all together. The admin who keeps the wheels turning. The teammate who always shows up, even when they're tired.

We assume they know we appreciate them.

They don't.

They need to hear it.

I once had an employee named Christine. She wasn't flashy. She wasn't loud. But she was steady. She was the kind of person who kept the team grounded, who picked up the slack without complaint, who noticed when others were struggling and quietly offered to help.

One day during a particularly stressful week, I sent her a quick email: *"Just wanted you to know I see how hard you're working, and I appreciate you more than I probably say. Thank you for being the glue."*

She replied within minutes. *"Thank you so much for this. I've been having a really tough week and thought no one noticed."*

That's all it took.

Thirty seconds to type.

But it shifted something for her. And for me.

Because when we *see* each other - really see each other - we're reminded that we're not alone. That what we do matters. That *we* matter.

This isn't just anecdotal.

Recognition, especially when it's specific and timely, has been linked to higher engagement, stronger performance, and greater psychological well-being [11]. And yet, a Gallup poll found that nearly 65% of employees haven't received any form of recognition in the last seven days [12].

That's a lot of invisible effort.

A lot of people wondering, *"Does any of this matter?"*

And not just at work.

I think about the single mom juggling three jobs, the new kid in class, the person in recovery counting one more sober day, the veteran navigating civilian life, the trans teen trying to stay safe while being seen, the widower quietly going through the motions while the world moves on.

They don't need a parade.

They need eye contact.

A kind word.

A moment where someone notices.

"Hey, I see you!"

The more we practice this, the more connected we feel - not just to others, but to ourselves. Because every time we choose presence over distraction, empathy over assumption, recognition over indifference - we build the kind of world we want to live in.

We soften the edges.

We fill in the gaps.

We remind each other that we're human before we're roles, before we're job titles, before we're personas.

And here's the secret: the more you see others, the more you start to see *yourself*.

You realize you deserve the same attention, care, and presence you offer to everyone else. You start to notice when you're tired. When you're doing well. When you've been carrying more than anyone knows.

Being seen isn't just something we receive.

It's something we give.

And in the giving - we all get a little closer to whole.

The Gift of Being Seen

If there's one truth I've learned again and again - sometimes through joy, and sometimes through fire - it's this:

Being seen heals what being invisible breaks.

We live in a time when connection has never been more available - and yet, more of us are feeling emotionally adrift. And while it's tempting to point to technology or busyness, the truth is simpler and deeper: we've forgotten how much it matters to *truly notice* each other.

To not just see someone's name on a calendar invite, but to ask, *"How are you…really?"*

To not just walk by someone's desk or scroll past their post, but to pause long enough to reflect their humanness back to them.

In a 2022 study from the American Psychological Association, researchers found that small, everyday gestures, like checking in or expressing appreciation, were consistently underestimated in their impact. The people on the receiving end felt more cared for, more seen, and more valued than the giver expected [13].

That tells us something profound: the things we think are "too small to matter" often matter most.

And here's what's just as powerful: you don't need a title or a platform to be someone who sees.

You can be the quiet voice that says, *"I noticed how hard you worked on that."*

The kind face in the room that offers a nod of encouragement.

The open-hearted friend who doesn't try to fix, but simply sits beside someone in their messy middle.

You can be the one who says, *"I see you, and you don't have to earn my care."*

Because when we feel seen, not for our output, but for our being, something in us begins to settle. We soften. We breathe deeper. We stop overthinking our worth. We come home to ourselves.

And maybe that's what we're all really aching for.

Not applause. Not approval. But belonging. Safety. Connection.

So as you move forward, I want to leave you with this simple encouragement:

Don't underestimate your power to help someone feel visible.

Even a glance, a question, a pause can remind someone they matter.

Be that kind of mirror.

Not the one that demands polish, but the one that reflects dignity, care, and truth.

Because in a world full of curated images and surface-level chatter, *seeing someone*, and letting yourself be seen—is one of the most radical, healing things you can do.

STOP OVERTHINKING IT

PAUSE. REFLECT. APPLY.

What to Remember

- Being seen isn't about spotlight moments - it's about everyday gestures that say "I notice you" and "you matter."
- Disconnection thrives in assumption. Connection blooms in attention.
- You don't need the perfect words or grand gestures to make someone feel seen.
- Small actions - like listening, following up, or naming someone's strength - can change how they see themselves.
- When we let ourselves be seen, we model courage - and invite others to do the same.
- Visibility is not just external recognition. It's an internal knowing: *I am worthy of belonging as I am.*

Self-Reflection

Take a few moments to journal or speak aloud these questions. No need to rush - just meet yourself with curiosity:

1. Who are the people in my life that consistently make me feel seen? What do they do that makes that possible?
2. When was a time I felt truly recognized - not for what I *did*, but for who I *was*?
3. Where in my life do I still feel the need to hide or perform? What am I afraid people will see?
4. Who might be in my circle - family, friends, coworkers - who needs to feel more seen by me?
5. What does *being seen* mean to me now, and how has that changed over time?

Try This Strategy

The Name-It Note

Once a week, choose one person in your world - at work, at home, in your community - and name something you *see* in them.

You can write it in a note, text it, say it out loud, or send a quick voice message. Keep it simple and honest:

"I see how hard you're trying. It matters."
"You bring so much calm to our team, even when things get chaotic."
"Your creativity is contagious—and I'm grateful for it."
"You make people feel safe just by being you."

It might feel small. But research shows that recognition - especially when it's specific and personal - strengthens trust and increases emotional well-being [2].

You never know how much someone needed to hear it.

Conversation Starter

Use this in a team meeting, a dinner conversation, or even on a walk with a friend:

"What's something someone saw in you before you saw it in yourself?"

It's a question that builds connection, honors influence, and reminds us how powerful it is to be *noticed*.

Chapter 7

Presence Over Performance

Why being present beats being perfect in every relationship.

There was a time in my life when I believed my value came from being impressive. If I could say the right thing, do the right thing, and make it look effortless, then I'd be worthy - of respect, of connection, of belonging.

So I performed.

I perfected presentations down to the comma. I answered emails at lightning speed. I anticipated needs before anyone had to ask. I was the woman who always had it together. Or at least, that's what I wanted people to believe.

But beneath the polished delivery and rapid responses was a woman who was tired. Not just physically tired - but soul-tired. Because performance is exhausting. It demands a constant level of vigilance. It tells you to stay one step ahead, to hide the mess, to never let your guard down. And over time, it creates distance. Between you and the people you care about. Between you and the moments you're supposed to be living. Between you and your truest self.

I didn't realize how much of my life I'd spent performing until I started leading team retreats. I'd stand in front of a room full of people and say something like, *"Let's talk about what it means to be fully present."* And then I'd feel the irony hit me. Because while I was saying the words, I was mentally five steps ahead - watching the clock, reviewing the agenda, scanning the room for reactions. I wasn't fully there. I was managing the moment, not living it.

And then something would happen.

Someone would share something vulnerable - a story about burnout, or a breakdown they'd hidden, or the feeling of always falling short. And just like that, the room would shift. The posturing would drop. People would look up from their notebooks. The energy would soften.

Because real connection doesn't happen when we're perfect.

It happens when we're present.

I'll never forget the moment I really understood what presence over performance looked like. It was during the first year of my doctoral residency. We were sitting in a trust circle - no formal introductions, no resumes, no presentations. Just us. A bunch of bright, high-achieving, type-A adults who had spent most of our lives performing to prove we belonged.

In the center of the circle sat a simple plastic water bottle. That was our "sharing stick." When the bottle was passed to you, it was your turn to speak. And it didn't take long to figure out what that really meant.

The moment the bottle reached someone's hands, they'd pause. Their eyes would well up with water. And then… it would happen.

Tears.

Confessions.

Fears that had been silently eating at each of us.

"I don't know if I belong here."

"I'm afraid I'm not smart enough."

"I feel like I'm one mistake away from being exposed."

We all felt it. The vulnerability bomb. The moment the water bottle landed in your lap, the truth came out. And weirdly... beautifully... that was the point. Our professor, Dr. Anthony Kortens, had crafted this moment with intention. He knew what we didn't yet realize - that the pressure to be perfect was suffocating our potential. That we couldn't grow if we were too busy pretending we already had it all figured out.

Dr. Kortens taught us about Carol Dweck's work on growth mindset - the belief that our abilities and intelligence can be developed through dedication and effort, not fixed by talent or title [14]. But he didn't just teach it. He modeled it. He created a space where imperfection wasn't a weakness - it was an invitation. A doorway to community. A chance to connect.

And it worked.

Those circles built the foundation for friendships that have lasted years. Not because we were impressive - but because we were real. Present. Vulnerable. Together.

That residency didn't just challenge my thinking academically. It changed how I show up in every relationship - personally and professionally. It reminded me that nobody connects with your performance. They connect with your presence. With your story. With the shaky, sweaty, imperfect truth of who you are when the mask comes off.

That's where the magic happens.

And here's the research to back it up: Studies show that emotional presence, being fully engaged and emotionally available, significantly enhances trust, team performance, and relationship satisfaction [15,16]. When we allow ourselves to be seen, especially in moments of challenge or uncertainty, it opens the door for others to do the same. Vulnerability is contagious. But so is pretending. And we get to choose which one we bring into the room.

So the next time you're tempted to prove your worth, pause.

Presence is enough.

I carried what I learned in that residency circle into my work. Into my teaching, trainings, coaching and presentations. Into my everyday relationships. And the truth is, once you experience the power of presence, you can't unsee it. You start to notice the subtle ways people armor up. You begin to recognize the difference between someone who's performing a conversation and someone who's *in* it with you.

You also notice how much of our everyday communication is just noise.

Half-listening.

Head nods without heart.

Empty affirmations that don't go deeper than "I hear you."

But presence? Real, grounded, eye-contact, heart-on-the-table presence? That's rare. And when you feel it, it stays with you.

I've sat across from leaders who could deliver flawless strategy decks, who knew every number on their spreadsheet, but who couldn't look someone in the eye and say, *"I'm not sure how this will affect you, but I want to hear your thoughts."*

And I've coached professionals who felt like they had to be *on* all the time - perfect posture, perfect answers, perfect language - until they finally admitted, *"I'm exhausted trying to be what people expect."*

So many of us are tired. Not from work - but from the pressure to *perform* ourselves into being taken seriously. We're managing impressions instead of managing relationships. And over time, that gap between who we are and who we present ourselves to be? It becomes unbearable.

But presence closes the gap.

Presence is the act of saying: I'm here. I don't have it all figured out. But I care enough to show up fully.

And that matters more than you think.

Harvard researcher Amy Cuddy found that the most effective way to build trust isn't by leading with competence - it's by leading with *warmth* [17]. People want to know you care before they care what you know. That's not just soft talk - that's science. Connection trumps perfection.

And here's the paradox: when you stop trying to be perfect, you actually become more impactful.

Why?

Because people relax around you.

They stop bracing.

They start breathing.

They open up.

They tell the truth.

They trust you.

I've had teams go from guarded silence to honest dialogue in a matter of hours - not because I had a clever facilitation technique, but because I modeled presence. I shared my mistakes. I asked imperfect questions. I admitted when I didn't know something. And suddenly, the entire room softened.

One person's presence gives others permission to drop their guard.

That's what makes presence more powerful than performance.

Because performance is about impressing. But presence is about connecting.

And you can't do both at the same time.

So whether you're leading a team, sitting across from a friend, walking into a boardroom, or tucking your kid into bed - remember this:

You don't need the perfect words.

You don't need to posture, polish, or prove.

You just need to *be* there.

Because people don't remember our best performance.

They remember when we showed up.

Maybe you're thinking right now:

Okay, Jolene, but what does that actually look like?

How do I stop performing and start being present when the room feels heavy, or the stakes feel high, or my brain won't stop spinning?

I get it. I've been there.

So, come with me for a minute.

Imagine you're about to walk into a conversation that matters.

Maybe it's a team meeting.

Maybe it's coffee with a friend you haven't seen in months.

Maybe it's just sitting at the dinner table after a long, exhausting day.

Take a slow breath.

Let your shoulders drop an inch. (You might not have even realized they were up near your ears.)

Before you open your mouth, before you pick up your phone, before you default to the script you always use - pause.

And ask yourself, quietly, gently:

What do I want them to feel after this conversation?

Not: *What do I want them to think about me?*

Not: *How do I say it perfectly?*

Not: *What's the smartest thing I could contribute?*

But: *What do I want them to feel?*

Safe?

Heard?

Valued?

Like they're not alone?

Start there.

Presence isn't about saying all the right things.

It's about *setting the right intention* before you say anything at all.

And when you feel yourself drifting back into old habits - the urge to impress, to polish, to prove - come back to that simple question.

What do I want them to feel?

Because when your focus is connection, not perfection, you naturally show up differently.

You soften.

You listen more.

You breathe more.

You stop performing the conversation - and you start living it.

And the truth is, most people don't remember the dazzling thing you said.

Connection > Performance

They remember how your presence made them feel.

Warm.

Seen.

Respected.

Understood.

Cared for.

That's the real magic.

And you already have it in you.

You don't need a new script.

You just need a new starting place: the heart.

When the Stakes are High

And maybe right now you're thinking -

That's great, but what about when the stakes feel high?

You know the feeling.

You're about to walk into a big meeting.

Or present to a group.

Or have a conversation you've been dreading.

Your heart is racing. Your mouth's gone dry.

And suddenly, all that "just be present" advice sounds easier said than done.

Believe me, I get it.

So here's what I want you to try, if you're willing:

Instead of rehearsing every possible word you might say…

Instead of trying to armor up and sound smarter, stronger, or more "together" than you feel…

Pause.

Put your hand flat against your chest for a second, if you can.

Feel your heartbeat.

You're here.

You're real.

You don't need to be perfect.

You just need to be *with* the people in front of you.

Before you say a word, set one tiny anchor in your mind:

"I'm not here to perform. I'm here to connect."

That's it.

Not to impress.

Not to defend.

Not to outsmart.

To connect.

Presence isn't about pushing through the fear - it's about bringing your heart with you, fear and all.

And strangely? That fear gets quieter when you stop fighting it. When you make it a companion, not an enemy.

(*You're nervous because you care.* That's a beautiful thing.)

So the next time you stand up to speak, or sit down for a hard conversation, remember:

Connection first.

Performance never.

When There's Conflict

And what about conflict?

What about those moments where presence feels the hardest - when you're frustrated, hurt, or trying to hold it together without shutting down?

If that's where you are, hear me when I say this:

You don't have to be perfect at handling hard conversations.

You just have to stay human inside them.

When emotions run high - whether it's yours or theirs - there's always a tiny moment, a fraction of a second, where you get to choose:

Am I going to react?

Or am I going to stay present?

It won't feel easy.

But it will feel worth it.

If you're facing conflict and you feel yourself starting to armor up - getting defensive, gearing up to shut down or "win" the conversation - try this simple move:

Mentally step back, just half a step.

Ask yourself one question:

"What is this really about?"

Not what the words are saying on the surface.

Not the tone that stings your pride.

But underneath all that - what is this really about?

Most of the time, it's about feeling unseen.

Unheard.

Unsafe.

Unvalued.

Theirs.

Yours.

Sometimes both.

Presence lets you listen for what's underneath, not just what's coming at you.

And even if you don't have the perfect comeback or a brilliant resolution in the moment, just *staying in it* - staying open, staying willing - is powerful enough to shift the entire conversation.

Sometimes the most healing thing you can do in conflict isn't to fix it right away.

It's to stay.

To not run.

To not turn your heart away.

That's presence.

Sometimes the greatest test of presence isn't how we show up for ourselves - it's how we show up for someone else when they're breaking open right in front of us.

It's in those raw, unscripted moments where our instinct is to rush in, smooth it over, make it okay.

But real connection asks for something different.

Something quieter.

Something harder.

Something so much more powerful.

You Don't Have to Fix It to Be Enough

And it's stronger than any perfect argument.

And maybe the hardest place to practice presence is when someone else is falling apart in front of you.

It's so tempting, isn't it?

To rush in with advice.

To try to fix it.

To wrap it up neatly so nobody has to feel too much for too long.

I get it.

I've done it more times than I can count.

Especially in leadership, or as a parent, or just as someone who loves deeply - you want to help. You want to say the right thing that makes it better. You want to scoop up the hurt and make it disappear.

But presence asks something different from us.

It asks us to stay.

Not to fix.

Not to solve.

Not to strategize.

Just to stay.

When someone else is hurting, and you're sitting across from their pain, the most powerful thing you can offer is your quiet, steady being.

A soft nod that says, *I'm not leaving.*

An open posture that says, *You're not a burden.*

A breath that says, *You don't have to hurry up and be okay.*

You don't have to find the perfect words.

You don't have to tell a story about a time you felt the same.

You don't have to "make it better."

In fact, neuroscience tells us that one of the most regulating things for a stressed nervous system isn't advice - it's *co-regulation* [18].

It's one regulated person staying calm, present, and steady while the other person processes their emotion.

In simple terms: **your calm can help calm someone else.**

You don't have to say anything profound.

You just have to stay.

Presence isn't about offering solutions.

It's about offering *yourself*.

A while back, a friend of mine was going through something heavy. Loss layered on top of loss. She didn't need my ideas. She didn't need my pep talks. She just needed to not be alone in it.

So we sat.

We ate takeout on the couch.

We watched bad TV.

We cried a little.

We laughed a little.

And every once in a while, she'd say, *"I'm so sorry - I'm a mess."*

And every time, I'd say, *"You don't owe me anything. You're allowed to be wherever you are."*

That's presence.

No performance.

No timeline for healing.

No expectation that you pull yourself together to make me comfortable.

It's saying with everything in you:

You're safe with me. You're still loved here.

And isn't that what we're all craving, when we're honest?

Not advice.

Not judgment.

Not a five-step plan.

Just someone willing to stay.

And the beautiful thing is:

When you practice presence like that for others, it teaches you how to offer it to yourself, too.

When you're having your own hard day, you'll hear the echo of that steady voice:

"You're safe here. You're still loved here. You don't have to hurry up and be okay."

And if you ask me, that's what real connection is made of.

Not perfect words.

Not perfect solutions.

Just presence.

Patient, steady, enough.

The Power of Just Showing Up

Presence won't always feel flashy.

It won't always earn applause or look impressive from the outside.

There will be no gold stars for staying steady when the room feels heavy.

No standing ovation for saying, *"I don't have the perfect words, but I'm here."*

But presence will leave a mark deeper than anything performance ever could.

It will be the thing people remember years later - not what you said, but *how you stayed.*

How you didn't flinch when they needed you most.

How you held space, instead of holding judgment.

How you chose connection over control.

And presence has a way of rippling outward.

When you stay, others feel safer to stay too.

When you soften, others can lay down their armor too.

When you choose to be real, even in the messy middle, you give others permission to be real too.

This isn't about becoming a *"perfectly present"* person.

This is about remembering, moment by messy moment, that the greatest thing you can offer isn't a polished version of yourself.

It's your heart.

It's your attention.

It's your willingness to stay real - even when it's hard.

You don't have to perform for belonging.

You belong as you are.

And when you show up like that - for yourself and for others - you don't just change conversations.

You change relationships.

You change rooms.

You change lives.

Including your own.

Because when you show up real, you don't just change rooms - you change hearts.

STOP OVERTHINKING IT

PAUSE. REFLECT. APPLY.

What to Remember

Presence isn't about having the right words, the right timing, or the right presentation.

It's about being willing to stay human in the moments that tempt you to armor up.

It's about connection over control.

Compassion over performance.

Realness over polish.

And the most powerful thing you can offer - whether you're leading a meeting, comforting a friend, navigating conflict, or sitting quietly with your own hard feelings - is your steady, imperfect, wholehearted presence.

You are enough just by showing up.

Self-Reflection

Pause here. Breathe. Let's look inward for a moment.

Choose a few of these questions and either sit with them quietly or journal your responses. Let this be a conversation with yourself, not a checklist to "get right."

- When do I feel most tempted to perform instead of simply being present?
- Where in my life am I still believing that I have to "earn" belonging through perfection?
- What does it feel like in my body when I'm truly present with someone?
- (Grounded? Open? Calm? Nervous but honest?)
- Who in my life makes me feel seen and safe without expecting me to be perfect?
- How can I learn from the way they show up?
- When was a time someone else's simple presence made a difference for me?

Try This Strategy

The 3-Breath Reset

The next time you feel yourself slipping into "performance mode" - whether before a meeting, during a tough conversation, or when you're tempted to retreat behind polish - try this:

1. **Pause.**
2. Put both feet flat on the ground. Notice the weight of your body being supported.
3. **Breathe.**

4. Take three slow, full breaths. Feel your chest rise and fall. Let your shoulders drop.
5. **Reconnect.**
6. Quietly remind yourself: *"I'm here to connect, not perform."*

Let presence become a practice, not a performance.

You don't have to get it perfect.

You just have to come back to yourself - again and again.

Conversation Starter

Want to invite deeper presence with your team, your family, your friends?

Here's a simple, brave prompt to try:

When someone's really present with you - what do they do that makes you feel safe or seen?

It's not about grand gestures.

It's about learning the small, powerful ways we can show up better for each other.

Keep in mind…

Presence isn't something you master once.

It's something you choose, moment by moment, breath by breath, relationship by relationship.

And every time you choose it - even imperfectly - you're changing the world around you in ways you may never fully see.

But trust me: it matters.

You matter.

Stay present.

PART III

WHERE IT ALL HAPPENS

Chapter 8

The Workplace is a Relationship Lab

How to stop overthinking your role and start showing up as a human.

There was a time when I thought professionalism meant perfection.

I believed that every word, every email, every meeting had to be carefully crafted - polished, strategic, bulletproof. I thought my credibility depended on never letting the messy, human parts of me show. So I played the role. I spoke when I was sure. I smiled when I was tired. I kept conversations safe, polished, appropriate. I stayed in the lines.

And for a while, it worked.

At least, it looked like it was working.

I moved up. I earned trust. I got the promotions.

But inside, I was tired - the kind of tired that a vacation doesn't fix.

Because performing all day, every day, is exhausting.

It wasn't until years later that I realized:

The workplace isn't a stage. It's a relationship lab.

It's not a place to perfect yourself - it's a place to practice being human.

To try. To connect. To learn how to show up with curiosity, with presence, with grace - even when it's hard.

And the real magic?

The workplace gives you hundreds of little opportunities to practice every single day.

Not perfectly.

Not impressively.

But authentically.

And when you stop overthinking your role - who you're supposed to be, how you're supposed to sound, what you're supposed to say...

you start discovering the real skill that sets you apart:

the ability to connect as a human first.

At its core, every workplace is a living, breathing web of relationships.

Between coworkers. Between teams. Between leaders and the people they serve.

And just like any relationship, they're messy.

They're full of hopes, assumptions, misunderstandings, quiet victories, unspoken fears, and the constant, invisible question running under every interaction:

Can I trust you?

Not:

Can I trust your résumé?

Can I trust your job title?

Can I trust your perfectly worded email?

But:

Can I trust that you're a real human, not just a role?

Can I trust that you'll see me - not just what I produce?

Can I trust that when things get hard, you won't just protect your image - you'll stay human, too?

When we overthink our roles, we start filtering everything through the lens of performance instead of presence.

We ask ourselves:

How do I sound smart enough?

How do I avoid saying the wrong thing?

How do I make sure they see me as competent, capable, impressive?

And slowly, without even realizing it, we build walls.

Walls made of buzzwords and polished responses.

Walls made of meetings where everyone nods but no one says what they really mean.

Walls that keep us from seeing - and being seen by - the very people we spend most of our waking hours with.

Overthinking turns connection into calculation.

And calculation kills trust.

Because the truth is:

You can't build real relationships from behind a mask.

Not at work.

Not anywhere.

How Overthinking Your Role Shrinks Connection

When we start overthinking who we're supposed to be at work, we stop showing up as who we actually are.

We slip into role-playing without even noticing:

- The polished leader.
- The agreeable teammate.
- The competent-but-distant manager.
- The always-busy employee who never asks for help.

And the more we overthink our role, the more we lose touch with the human underneath it.

We stop asking real questions.

We hesitate before offering honest feedback.

We mute parts of ourselves that feel "too much" or "not enough."

We shrink our personality to fit the perception we think others want.

We second-guess whether it's even okay to just be... us.

It's subtle.

It's slow.

And it's devastating.

Because real connection - the kind that builds belonging, psychological safety, and high-performing teams - doesn't happen in the spaces where people are perfectly performing their roles.

It happens in the messy, human moments where walls come down.

Where people admit, *"I'm stuck."*

Where leaders say, *"I don't have all the answers, but I'm here to figure it out with you."*

Where coworkers notice, *"Hey, you've been quiet lately - you good?"*

Overthinking doesn't just make you feel alone.

It makes everyone around you feel a little more alone, too.

Because when we're performing, not connecting, we're signaling to others:

Stay guarded. Stay polished. Stay safe.

And workplaces filled with guarded, polished, "safe" people?

They don't innovate.

They don't collaborate deeply.

They don't build the kind of trust that can weather hard seasons.

They look fine on the surface - but underneath?

People are quietly disengaged.

Quietly lonely.

Quietly aching for something more real.

Overthinking shrinks connection because it shrinks courage.

And courage - even tiny, everyday doses of it - is what keeps relationships alive.

How Workplaces Thrive When Humans (Not Roles) Show Up

When we stop overthinking our roles and start showing up as humans, everything changes.

Workplaces aren't made stronger by flawless job descriptions or tightly defined responsibilities. They're made stronger by people.

People who care. People who connect. People who notice and respond in real time - not just according to the handbook.

When we show up as whole people, not just job titles, we build trust faster.

We collaborate more honestly.

We catch problems sooner.

We support each other better.

Because humans notice things roles don't.

Roles can deliver results.

Humans deliver relationships.

And relationships are what sustain organizations through change, challenge, and uncertainty.

I've seen it firsthand.

The teams that thrive aren't the ones with the flashiest mission statements or the most polished org charts.

They're the ones where people remember that every project, every meeting, every process is carried by actual living, breathing humans - with hopes, stresses, talents, and struggles.

They're the ones where someone says,

"Hey, you look a little off today. Want to grab five minutes after this?"

Or,

"I know you're great at details. Would you mind helping me double-check this before we send it out?"

Or even,

"I'm nervous about this presentation - could you sit up front so I have a friendly face to look at?"

These don't sound like radical moves.

They sound simple.

Almost too simple.

But simple is where connection lives.

Simple is what keeps people from burning out quietly.

Simple is what builds a safety net under ambition and innovation and all the big, shiny things workplaces say they want more of.

Because when people feel seen, they contribute more.

When they feel trusted, they risk more.

When they feel cared about, they stay longer.

Humans first.

Always.

I once coached a manager named Laura who told me she was afraid to overstep her role.

She said, *"I'm the team lead, not their therapist. I don't want to cross boundaries."*

And while that caution came from a good place, it was keeping her stuck.

She wasn't asking how people were really doing. She wasn't offering encouragement unless it related strictly to a deliverable.

Her team respected her - but they didn't trust her.

And trust is what moves teams from compliance to commitment.

When Laura finally gave herself permission to *show up as a human* - to acknowledge someone's hard day, to celebrate small wins, to admit when she was struggling too - everything shifted.

Performance improved.

Collaboration deepened.

The invisible wall between "leader" and "team" softened into a bridge.

Overthinking shrinks connection.

Humanity expands it.

When we trust ourselves to be real - not reckless, not boundary-less, but real - we invite others to do the same.

And that's when workplaces stop feeling like battlegrounds and start feeling like communities.

Permission to Be a Person, Not Just a Performer

he hardest part about shifting from "role mode" to "human mode" isn't that it's complicated.

It's that it feels unfamiliar.

We've been trained, often for years, to lead with our title, our task list, or our performance reviews.

You introduce yourself by your job, not your joy.

You measure your day by your output, not your connection.

You value yourself by how much you checked off, not how you showed up for others - or yourself.

And slowly, without even realizing it, you start living like a résumé instead of a relationship.

But here's the truth:

You were never hired just to fill a role.

You were hired because someone believed you—your perspective, your presence, your approach - would add value.

You are the magic.

Not your job description.

Not your metrics.

You.

When we remember that, we show up differently.

We stop treating meetings like transactions.

We start treating them like opportunities - to listen, to notice, to encourage, to collaborate.

And connection doesn't slow down results - it fuels them.

In fact, according to a report from BetterUp, employees who experience high levels of belonging at work see a 56% increase in job performance, a 50% drop in turnover risk, and a 75% reduction in sick days [19].

Belonging isn't a "nice to have."

It's rocket fuel for real results.

But we can't create belonging if everyone's trapped behind polished performances, walking around as titles instead of teammates.

So permission granted:

- You can be a person, not just a performer.
- You can bring your humanity into the room.
- You can lead, influence, contribute—not by having all the right answers, but by being fully, presently you.

Signs You're Overthinking Your Role (And Shrinking Connection)

Overthinking your role doesn't always show up as obvious anxiety.

Sometimes it's subtle - but it still quietly shrinks your ability to connect.

Here are a few signs to watch for:

- You rehearse conversations in your head before casual meetings.
- You over-edit your words before you even say them.
- You ask yourself, "Is this my place to say something?" - and then stay silent.
- You worry about stepping outside your lane, so you hold back genuine contributions.
- You constantly monitor how you're being perceived.
- You scan every interaction, wondering if you came across as smart enough, polished enough, senior enough.
- You delay outreach or follow-ups because you're "not ready yet."
- You convince yourself you need the perfect message, the perfect moment, the perfect wording - so connection gets delayed (or disappears altogether).

- You stick strictly to your job description - even when your instincts say someone needs human care.
- You tell yourself, "That's not my role," even when it's a moment where kindness, acknowledgment, or simple humanity would mean more than any official task.

None of this makes you a bad employee.

It just means you're stuck in your head - trying so hard to perform the role well that you're missing the invitation to be a real, imperfect, present human being.

And ironically?

The more you overthink your role, the harder it becomes to actually thrive in it.

Because leadership, collaboration, trust, and growth?

They don't happen role-to-role.

They happen human-to-human.

Connection Happens Human-to-Human, Not Role-to-Role

We don't connect with titles.

We connect with people.

No one says, *"Wow, the Senior Data Analyst position really changed my life."*

They say, *"I'll never forget how Sam made me feel seen when I was struggling."*

Or, *"Maria was the first person who really believed in me at work."*

In other words:

It's not your position that leaves a lasting impact.

It's your presence.

When you overthink your role, you focus on the mechanics:

What's my authority here? How do I stay in my lane? Am I being "professional" enough?

And in doing so, you risk missing the moments that matter most - the ones that aren't about hierarchy or formality, but about humanity.

The truth is, the best workplaces aren't built by flawless execution alone.

They're built by the quiet, everyday choices people make to show up for each other as human beings - not just as job descriptions.

Like pausing to ask a teammate how they're really doing after a tough meeting.

Or remembering something personal they shared last week - and checking in on it.

Or offering encouragement when someone doubts themselves, even if it's outside your "official" responsibilities.

These small human moments don't show up on the org chart.

They don't get a line item on a performance evaluation.

But they shape everything about how a workplace feels - and how people show up inside it.

Because connection isn't role-dependent.

It's humanity-dependent.

When we default to role-over-relationship thinking - "I'm just their peer," "I'm just an admin," "I'm just the new hire" - we shrink our impact without even realizing it.

We miss opportunities to lead, to care, to build trust.

But when we lead with humanity first - no matter what our job title says - we create a kind of workplace magic that can't be mandated in policy.

The best teams, the best leaders, the best workplaces?

They don't just tolerate humanity.

They celebrate it.

They understand that the strongest teams aren't made of perfect resumes - they're made of imperfect humans who are willing to connect, care, and grow together.

And that doesn't require a title.

It just requires you to show up.

You Don't Have to Be the CEO to Change the Culture

Culture isn't created at the top. It's created in the middle.

When people talk about workplace culture, they usually point upward.

"If leadership would just…"

"If management understood…"

"If HR actually cared…"

But here's the truth most people miss:

Culture isn't something leaders *create* and hand down.

It's something that lives and breathes in the middle of the organization - between people.

Yes, leadership sets the tone.

Yes, policies matter.

But the **daily experience** of culture comes from the hundreds of tiny interactions between colleagues, customers, clients, and teams.

It comes from how we treat each other when no one's watching.

It lives in the micro-moments:

- How you greet someone in the hallway.
- Whether you listen to understand, or just to reply.
- Whether you advocate for someone's idea in a meeting when they aren't in the room.
- Whether you ask the awkward question instead of pretending you know.

Culture isn't built through memos and mission statements.

It's built through *moments*.

And moments belong to everyone because micro-moments shape macro outcomes.

It's tempting to think that small actions don't matter.

That saying "thank you" one more time or asking how someone's day is going is just...nice, but inconsequential.

But research proves otherwise.

According to a study in *Harvard Business Review*, small positive interactions at work - simple moments of recognition, empathy, and connection - are one of the strongest predictors of team engagement and resilience [20].

Why?

Because small moments send big messages:

"You belong here."

"Your effort matters."

"You're not invisible."

And those messages?

They stack up.

They shape how people feel about their work, their team, and themselves.

Think about the best teams you've been part of.

Were they the smartest teams?

The most efficient?

Maybe.

But chances are, they were the teams where you *felt safe enough* to be yourself.

Where someone noticed you.

Where someone listened.

Where someone had your back.

That feeling doesn't happen by accident.

It's built - moment by moment - by people who choose connection over convenience.

And the best part?

You don't need permission to start.

You Are Culture

If you're part of the workplace, you *are* part of the culture.

Period.

Every interaction is a brick in the foundation.

Every email. Every check-in. Every hallway conversation.

It's all building something - even if no one's handing you blueprints.

And here's where the shift happens:

You can either be a passive participant - shaped by the culture around you.

Or you can be an active creator - shaping the culture you want to live in.

You don't have to be the CEO.

You don't have to have a fancy title.

You just have to choose to show up differently - even when it feels like no one else is.

Because sometimes the single biggest change in a culture starts with one person asking a different question.

One person staying curious in conflict.

One person slowing down to listen.

One person being real instead of rehearsed.

When you choose connection over performance, you shift the energy around you.

And energy is contagious - for better or worse.

The small things you do ripple outward in ways you may never see.

But trust me: they matter.

You're a culture-maker whether you realize it or not.

Every choice you make - to be present, to ask, to notice, to listen - is culture-making.

So is every choice to disengage, dismiss, or default to performance.

You are either reinforcing the culture you inherited -

or you're building something better, brick by brick.

And while it might not always be visible right away -

while it might feel slow or even invisible at times -

it's still happening.

Someone feels a little more seen because of you.

Someone dares to speak up because of you.

Someone chooses to stay because of you.

That's leadership.

That's culture-building.

And you don't need a title to do it.

You just need the willingness to show up human.

Again and again.

Overthinking Your Role Shrinks Connection

When we start overthinking our role - whether it's our job title, our responsibilities, or our "place" in the room - something sneaky happens:

We shrink.

Not physically.

Not obviously.

But emotionally.

Relationally.

We start filtering every interaction through the lens of "Is this my place?" instead of "How can I connect here?"

- We hesitate to offer encouragement because it's "not our role."
- We stay silent when we have a good idea because "someone else probably has it covered."
- We withhold kindness because "I'm just an admin," or "I'm not their boss," or "They barely know me."

We start playing small, waiting for permission to be human.

And the more we shrink ourselves down to our job description, the less human we become - to ourselves and to others.

Because humans don't connect through titles.

They connect through presence.

Performance Over Presence: How Overthinking Erodes Trust

When you overthink your role, you start treating every interaction like a performance review.

You're constantly scanning:

- Is this appropriate?
- Will this make me look good?
- Am I staying in my lane?

And slowly, relationships turn transactional instead of transformational.

It's subtle, but deadly to connection:

Instead of genuine conversation, you get cautious compliance.

Instead of creative collaboration, you get careful calculation.

Instead of mutual trust, you get mutual performance.

People sense when you're guarded.

They sense when you're managing impressions instead of offering yourself.

And the tragedy is:

You have so much more to offer than your role.

Your ideas. Your curiosity. Your humor. Your empathy.

All the best parts of you get locked behind a wall of "professionalism" that no one asked you to build.

Keep in mind that true professionalism is human.

Professionalism isn't about being perfect.

It's not about knowing every answer or following every unwritten rule of hierarchy.

True professionalism is about being human in a way that builds trust.

It's knowing your stuff and knowing how to listen.

It's speaking up when something matters and staying curious when you don't have the full story.

It's honoring your responsibilities without sacrificing your humanity.

The best workplaces aren't the ones where everyone stays in their little silo and colors inside the lines.

The best workplaces are the ones where people show up as whole humans first - not just job titles.

Because when people feel seen, valued, and trusted beyond their role, they do better work.

They stay longer.

They take risks.

They care.

And all of that starts with one shift:

Stop overthinking your role.

Start showing up as a human.

How to Show Up Human Without Overstepping

Now, showing up as a whole human doesn't mean throwing professionalism out the window.

It doesn't mean treating every meeting like a therapy session or forgetting your role altogether.

There's a difference between **being human** and **being unfiltered**.

So how do you show up with heart *without* crossing boundaries or making others uncomfortable?

Here's the simple guide I use - whether I'm leading a team, teaching a class, coaching executives, or just navigating everyday relationships:

1. Lead with Curiosity, Not Assumption

When in doubt, ask instead of assume.

"Is there anything I can do to support you?"

"Would it help if I shared a few ideas, or would you prefer space to think it through?"

"Is now a good time to check in, or should we circle back later?"

Curiosity signals respect.

It gives people a choice.

It shows that you're there *for them*, not for yourself.

2. Match the Moment, Not the Mood

If someone's frustrated, you don't have to immediately dive into problem-solving mode.

If someone's celebrating, you don't have to be the voice of caution and logistics.

Showing up human means being attuned to the emotional moment - not trying to control it.

- Celebrate with the celebrators.
- Listen to the grievers.
- Breathe with the stressed.

Presence matters more than precision.

3. Offer, Don't Override

When you're building trust and connection, offering matters more than directing.

Instead of jumping in with solutions or advice, try softer language:

"Would it be helpful if I...?"

"Would you like me to share an observation?"

"I have a thought — want me to throw it out there?"

This small shift moves you from **fixer** to **partner**.

It keeps the door open for real conversation - without steamrolling someone's agency.

4. Stay Rooted in Respect

Being human doesn't mean abandoning good judgment.

- Confidentiality still matters.
- Personal boundaries still matter.
- Timing still matters.

If someone isn't ready to open up - respect that.

If a meeting calls for focus, stay focused.

If a boundary is drawn, honor it.

Real connection is never forced.

It's invited.

Quick Litmus Test: Human, or Overstepping?

Before you share, support, or step in - pause and ask:

- Am I acting from connection or from my own discomfort?
- Am I offering, or am I assuming?
- Am I respecting their pace, or trying to move faster than they're ready for?

If you're rooted in curiosity, respect, and presence - you're on solid ground.

Why Workplaces That Allow Humanity Outperform Those That Prioritize Polish

Here's what I've seen again and again - in coaching leaders, training teams, and leading organizations myself:

The most effective, resilient workplaces aren't the ones obsessed with looking perfect.

They're the ones that create space for people to be *real.*

Because when people feel like they have to wear a mask to be taken seriously —

they hold back.

They second-guess.

They stay surface-level.

They stay safe.

And when people are stuck in safe mode, you lose:

- Creativity
- Innovation
- Courage
- Deep collaboration
- Honest feedback
- True commitment

On the surface, things might look "professional" - clean, polished, conflict-free.

But underneath?

There's a quiet disengagement happening.

A slow erosion of trust.

A withering of potential.

Polish without presence always costs you.

On the other hand - when workplaces make it safe for humans to show up?

When they reward honesty over optics, effort over image, growth over appearance?

Everything changes.

- People share ideas *before* they're fully formed - so innovation speeds up.
- Conflicts surface *earlier* and get resolved *healthier* - so relationships strengthen.
- Mistakes are owned *faster* and learned from *quicker* - so growth accelerates.
- Feedback flows more *freely* - so trust compounds.
- Collaboration deepens - because people aren't just aligning their roles. They're aligning their hearts.

And guess what?

The results follow.

According to research from Google's Project Aristotle, the highest-performing teams had one thing in common:

Not the smartest people.

Not the most experienced people.

Not the most polished people.

Psychological safety [21].

That's it.

The feeling that says:

"I can speak up here."

"I can show up here."

"I can stumble here - and still belong."

And psychological safety isn't built by perfection.

It's built by presence.

Quick Snapshot:

Workplace Prioritizing Polish	Workplace Prioritizing Humanity
Fear of mistakes	Freedom to learn
Surface-level communication	Honest conversations
Hidden conflict	Healthy resolution
Burnout from constant performance	Engagment through real connection
Retention struggles	Loyalty and growth

Real-World Proof That Humanity Wins

I know it can sound idealistic to say *"just be human"* at work.

So let's get practical. Let's get real.

I've walked into organizations where performance ruled everything - where people were so afraid to make a mistake that innovation flatlined. Where conflict simmered under the surface until it exploded. Where people left not because the work was too hard, but because the relationships were too hollow.

And I've seen the opposite too.

I've seen what happens when leaders and teammates dare to show up differently. When they choose authenticity over appearance. When they choose presence over posturing. When they choose to connect like human beings first, and professionals second.

Here's what it looks like in real life:

- A CEO who kicks off town halls not with metrics, but by sharing a real story of a recent challenge - and what it taught her.
- A manager who responds to a missed deadline not with shame, but with a curious question: *"What got in the way?"*
- A team that pauses after a tough project not just to debrief the deliverables, but to ask, *"How are we feeling after that?"*
- A leader who says, *"I don't have all the answers, but I trust this team to figure it out together."*
- A colleague who notices when someone's off their game and sends a genuine, simple message: *"I'm here if you need anything."*

These aren't grand gestures.

They're micro-moments.

But they change everything.

In workplaces where humanity leads:

- Mistakes become learning moments instead of career death sentences.
- Honest conversations become the norm, not the exception.
- Trust deepens because people know they're valued for who they are - not just what they produce.

And the ripple effect?

- Engagement goes up.
- Creativity comes back.
- Loyalty strengthens.

People don't leave workplaces where they feel seen, heard, and valued.

They leave workplaces where they're treated like a cog in the machine.

You don't have to overhaul your company culture overnight.

You don't have to have a perfect plan.

You just have to start - one human, one conversation, one moment at a time.

Practical Move to Show Up Human at Work

So how do you actually do this?

How do you stop overthinking your role, your title, your reputation - and start showing up as a human being who leads with connection?

You don't need a personality transplant.

You don't need to share your whole life story at every meeting.

You don't even need to be the loudest voice in the room.

You just need a few intentional shifts.

Here's where you can start:

1. Lead with Curiosity, Not Assumptions.

Before you jump to conclusions about a colleague's reaction, decision, or silence - pause. Ask, *"I noticed you were quiet in that meeting - anything on your mind?"* or *"Tell me more about how you see this."*

Curiosity opens doors. Assumptions close them.

2. Acknowledge, Don't Just Evaluate.

Catch people doing things *right*.

Instead of waiting for performance reviews or milestones, build tiny moments of recognition into everyday work.

"I really appreciated how you handled that tricky client call."

"Your perspective helped me see that differently."

3. Show Your Real Reactions.

You don't need to armor up all the time.

If you're moved by someone's vulnerability, say it. If you're excited about an idea, show it. Let your team feel your *real* energy - not just your professional poker face.

4. Share Progress, Not Just Perfection.

Model what it looks like to be a work-in-progress.

In a team meeting, try something simple like: *"Here's where I'm still wrestling with this - I'd love your input."*

When you normalize learning *out loud,* others feel safer doing the same.

5. Set a Human Intention for Each Interaction.

Before a meeting, email, or conversation, quickly ask yourself:

"Am I trying to impress - or connect?"

Let connection guide you. It shifts your tone, your words, even your body language.

6. Make Room for Emotions Without Making It About You.

When someone shares frustration, fear, or sadness, resist the urge to immediately problem-solve or redirect the conversation.

Stay with them.

A simple, *"That sounds really hard - thank you for trusting me with that,"* goes a long way.

7. Celebrate Small Moments of Humanity.

I'll admit - I'm a big fan of celebrating the small things. I've found this to be on of the biggest game-changers in shifting how people feel.

If someone was honest about needing help? Celebrate that.

A teammate admitted a mistake? Celebrate that.

Every time you recognize these moments instead of rushing past them, you build a culture where presence matters more than polish.

Quick Reminder:

You don't have to nail all of this at once.

You don't have to "be better at being human" overnight.

You're already human.

This is just about letting that humanity lead a little more visibly, a little more intentionally, one moment at a time.

Bringing It All Together

If there's one thing I hope you take away from this chapter - and this entire book - it's this:

You're not a role.

You're not a résumé.

You're not a performance to be graded.

You're a human being.

And the greatest gift you bring to any workplace, any relationship, any room - is exactly that: your humanity.

Not your perfection.

Not your polish.

Not your ability to fit a mold or tick every box.

Your ability to be present.

To see and be seen.

To connect.

To care.

And here's the beautiful irony:

When you stop overthinking your role, you actually become *better* at it.

When you lead with heart instead of hustle, people trust you more.

When you show up real instead of rehearsed, people lean in instead of pulling away.

You create the kind of culture where people feel safe to bring their best - not because they're performing for approval, but because they feel like they *belong.*

And that, more than any metric or milestone, is what builds lasting success - in work, in leadership, and in life.

So as you move forward, remember:

You don't have to perform to belong.

You don't have to overthink every move to be valuable.

You don't have to become someone else to be enough.

You already are.

You belong here - as you.

You're ready for deeper connection - right now.

And the workplaces, teams, and relationships you're a part of?

They're ready for you too.

The real you.

The human you.

The one who's been enough all along.

Let's build that kind of world together - one real, messy, beautifully human moment at a time.

STOP Overthinking It

Pause. Reflect. Apply.

What to Remember

Your workplace is not just a place to perform - it's a place to practice connection.

Overthinking your role shrinks your impact; showing up as a human expands it.

Presence, not polish, is what people trust and remember.

You already have everything you need to build real belonging - just by being yourself.

Self-Reflection

Take a moment to sit with these questions:

1. Where have I been overthinking my role instead of showing up as myself?
2. What part of my real, human self do I want to bring forward more at work?
3. How might my workplace feel different if I showed up 5% more present, more human, more real?

Try This Strategy

The Human Check-In

Before your next work interaction (meeting, email, conversation), pause and set this micro-intention:

> *"I'm not here to impress. I'm here to connect."*

Then show up accordingly - even if it's just a small shift.

Conversation Starter

Want to spark more human conversations at work? Try this simple prompt in a meeting, one-on-one, or team gathering:

> *"What's something you're proud of lately - even if it feels small?"*

It's an invitation for realness. And it just might change the tone of the entire room.

Chapter 9

Net-Weaving, Not Networking

How to Build Professional Relationships that Actually Feel Good.

There's a word that sends a surprising number of people into a spiral of overthinking:

Networking.

Even just hearing it can trigger an involuntary grimace.

Maybe you're picturing forced smiles, awkward name tag moments, and small talk that feels more like a performance than a conversation.

Or maybe you think of networking events where everyone seems polished, perfect, and ready with their elevator pitch - while you're just trying to figure out how to balance your drink, your plate, and your dignity.

You're not alone.

The traditional model of "networking" has left a lot of us feeling disillusioned - and disconnected.

It's no wonder: most of the advice we've been given about building professional relationships focuses on **transaction** over **connection**.

Collect the business cards.

Deliver the perfect elevator pitch.

Follow up with a strategic ask.

But that's not how real relationships - or real opportunities - are built.

In reality, the people who build the most meaningful, supportive, and opportunity-rich networks aren't **networkers** at all.

They're **net-weavers**.

They're the people who show up with **curiosity**, not a pitch.

The people who listen more than they talk.

The people who remember your story, not just your title.

They weave relationships the way you'd weave a basket - one strand of grass at a time, with care, attention, and genuine connection.

And here's the best part:

Anyone can do this.

You don't have to be extroverted.

You don't have to be polished.

You don't have to have a perfect LinkedIn profile.

You just have to show up **real**.

Net-weaving doesn't operate on the assumption that every conversation has to lead to something.

It works on a different belief:

Every person matters, even if there's no immediate "return on investment."

When you show up not to **get something** but to **build something**, people feel it.

It's disarming in the best way.

Instead of wondering, *"What do they want from me?"* they start thinking, *"Who is this person who's actually paying attention?"*

And that simple shift - from transaction to connection - changes everything.

Dr. Brené Brown often reminds us that true connection requires vulnerability, and vulnerability is impossible if we're treating relationships like checklists or scorecards.

In her words, *"Connection is the energy that exists between people when they feel seen, heard, and valued."*

That kind of energy can't be manufactured through a polished introduction.

It grows naturally through presence, curiosity, and care.

This is why I believe LinkedIn has evolved into one of the most powerful net-weaving platforms we have today.

Once seen as just a job-hunting site or an online résumé board, LinkedIn has become a living, breathing community.

It's a place where real conversations, real support, and real relationships unfold - if you approach it with a net-weaver's mindset.

Instead of asking, *"How can I leverage this person?"*

We ask, *"How can I learn from, support, or encourage this person?"*

Instead of thinking, *"What's the perfect post that will make me look good?"*

We think, *"What's something honest, helpful, or uplifting I can contribute?"*

And when you show up like that - real, interested, and willing to engage without a hidden agenda - people notice.

Because in a sea of self-promotion and surface-level connection, authenticity stands out like a lighthouse.

I see this play out every time I attend a conference or speak at an event.

After every session, there's the inevitable business card exchange - but I don't treat those cards like trophies.

I treat them like **story holders**.

After every conversation, I quietly jot down something specific about the person:

Maybe it's how we met ("bus shuttle to the convention center"), something funny they shared (like the woman who had to ditch her beloved high heels after a marathon check-in fiasco), or something that struck me about them.

Later, when I'm home, I don't just fire off a generic LinkedIn request.

I sit down and **write a handwritten note** - a real one.

Something that reflects what made them memorable.

Something that says: *"I didn't just meet you. I saw you."*

(And yes, I usually reference the red hair, the new shoes, or the impromptu shopping mall adventure if it made me laugh - because those human moments are what make the connection real.)

That small act doesn't just help me remember people.

It helps **them** feel remembered.

And in a world where so many people feel overlooked, that's a bigger gift than we realize.

Why Traditional Networking Feels So Cringey - and Why Net-Weaving Feels Better

Let's be honest:

Most traditional networking feels awkward at best, and downright soul-sucking at worst.

You know the drill.

You walk into a networking event, clutching a stack of business cards like armor.

You scan the room for someone - anyone - who doesn't already look deep in conversation.

You rehearse your elevator pitch in your head.

You make small talk about the weather, the venue, the traffic.

You wonder if you're supposed to ask for something directly, or if that makes you look desperate.

You nod politely while mentally counting the minutes until you can leave.

If that's what networking is supposed to feel like, it's no wonder so many of us dread it.

Traditional networking often feels cringey because it's rooted in performance, not presence.

It's transactional.

It's focused on what you can *get* rather than what you can *give*.

And most people can feel the difference immediately.

Maya Angelou captures this dynamic perfectly when she talks about the difference between fitting in and belonging.

She says:

> "True belonging doesn't require you to change who you are; it requires you to be who you are."
>
> — Maya Angelou

Traditional networking pressures us to fit in.

Net-weaving invites us to belong.

That's why net-weaving feels so much better - because it taps into what we actually crave:

Not more contacts.

More connection.

Instead of treating conversations like job interviews, net-weaving treats them like beginnings.

Instead of trying to impress, it seeks to understand.

Instead of focusing on outcomes, it focuses on people.

And here's the secret: **Net-weaving isn't just more humane - it's more effective.**

Research from Harvard Business Review shows that the strongest, most fruitful professional relationships are built not on opportunistic networking, but on genuine curiosity and mutual support [22].

People are much more likely to help, refer, recommend, or collaborate with people they trust - and trust isn't built in a 30-second elevator pitch.

It's built over time, through real moments of presence, listening, and care.

When you stop trying to impress and start trying to connect, people remember you.

Not because you had the perfect LinkedIn headline or the flashiest pitch,

but because you made them feel seen, valued, and important.

And in a world full of transactions, being remembered like that is rare - and powerful.

How Net-Weaving Feels Different

Networking often feels like a transaction.

- Hand over a business card.
- Exchange pleasantries.
- Follow up with a LinkedIn request that says, *"Let's stay connected!"* (but rarely actually connect.)

It's not that networking is bad. It's just that, for many of us, **it feels hollow** - like a script we're supposed to follow instead of a relationship we're excited to build.

Net-weaving, on the other hand, feels completely different.

It's relational, not transactional. It's about building real bridges, not tallying business cards.

Instead of asking:

"What can I get from you?"

You ask:

"How can I support you?"

"How can we support each other?"

Net-weaving shifts the entire energy.

It turns every interaction into an opportunity for curiosity, generosity, and shared growth.

One of my favorite examples of net-weaving came after a conference where I spoke about leadership and connection. Afterward, a woman came up to me, introduced herself, and instead of launching into her elevator pitch, she simply said:

"Your story about hiding behind achievement really resonated with me. It made me think about how much I've been doing that, too."

We found a quiet corner and started talking - not about resumes, but about real life.

She shared that for years, she had built her identity around professional accolades: certifications, promotions, leadership awards. From the outside, it looked like she was thriving. But inside, she was carrying an ache she couldn't quite name - a feeling that no matter how much she achieved, it was never enough.

She told me about a moment just a few weeks earlier: standing on stage receiving an award for Excellence in Leadership and feeling completely hollow inside. She smiled for the photos. She shook the hands. She gave the polished thank-you speech.

But later that night, back at home, she cried.

Not because she wasn't proud - but because she realized how far she had drifted from herself. From the parts of her life that didn't fit neatly into a LinkedIn headline.

"I didn't want another accolade," she said quietly. *"I wanted to feel like I mattered, even without a title next to my name."*

That conversation stayed with me long after the conference ended.

Because it was real.

It wasn't about networking. It wasn't about what we could *do* for each other.

It was about being human with each other.

We followed each other on LinkedIn that day - and years later, we're still connected, cheering each other on from different corners of the country.

Not because we needed something from each other.

But because we *saw* each other.

That's net-weaving.

It's about weaving a web of real connection, not just collecting contacts.

And you know what?

It lasts.

Transactional networks fade when they're no longer "useful."

But relational webs strengthen over time - even when you don't talk every day.

Because they were built on something deeper than mutual benefit.

They were built on mutual *care*.

Because real connection doesn't always happen in the moments we plan.

It happens in the small, unscripted moments - if we're willing to stay open.

I remember flying to a conference once, when I found myself sitting next to another attendee, Amy. We both had been upgraded to first class, and as we settled in, we struck up a conversation.

We quickly realized we were headed to the same event - both HR Directors, both juggling busy lives, both a little tired but looking forward to the conference ahead.

At one point, it was probably around one o'clock in the afternoon, and she glanced over, almost shyly, and asked,

"Would you like to get a glass of wine?"

We laughed, sharing that unspoken *"is it too early?"* look, and agreed: why not?

And over that simple glass of wine, a real connection began to form.

Not because we exchanged business cards first.

Not because we talked strategy or swapped résumés.

But because we shared a human moment.

We talked about travel mishaps and work pressures and the funny, messy realities of our jobs and our lives.

And that conversation - spontaneous, imperfect, and real - built a bridge that no perfectly polished elevator pitch ever could have. And we ended up hanging out for the duration of the conference - and it was magical. To this day, Amy and I still are fast friends and keep in touch.

That's what net-weaving is about.

It's not about collecting contacts for later use.

It's about noticing the moment you're in - and choosing to connect, human to human, heart to heart.

Because sometimes, the best professional relationships don't start with a handshake.

They start with a shared laugh.

A glass of wine at 30,000 feet.

A story about sore feet and a shopping mall detour.

Or a simple, *"Hey, me too."*

Why Net-Weaving is the Future of Real Leadership and Life Success

When we talk about relationships - professional or personal - it's easy to slip into old patterns.

In the workplace, it's easy to think relationships are simply about getting ahead, building your network, or having *"the right people"* in your corner.

In our personal lives, it's easy to think connection only happens at milestones - weddings, holidays, scheduled calls.

But here's what we're waking up to, as humans and as leaders:

Real relationships - the ones that fuel trust, collaboration, belonging, and meaning - aren't built on transactions.

They're built on presence.

On shared humanity.

On showing up without an agenda.

This is why net-weaving matters so much now.

Because the world doesn't need more polished LinkedIn profiles or curated highlight reels.

It needs more people who are willing to show up for each other - in the small moments *and* the big ones.

And research supports this shift.

A 2022 study published in *MIT Sloan Management Review* found that organizations with cultures rooted in authentic relationship-building - not just performance metrics - saw **higher employee retention, greater innovation,** and **stronger cross-functional collaboration** [23].

The same is true outside of work. In longitudinal studies on well-being, like the Harvard Study of Adult Development, relationships - genuine, supportive ones - were found to be the number one predictor of both physical health and happiness across a lifetime [24].

Not titles.

Not follower counts.

Not polished perfection.

Real connection.

We're moving from a world that rewards surface-level networking to one that requires depth.

We're realizing that the old model - shake hands, swap cards, move on - leaves people feeling hollow, not connected.

And that goes for friends, colleagues, neighbors, clients, and even strangers.

The new model is rooted in something far more powerful:

Attention. Care. Curiosity. Courage. Presence.

That's why when you're thinking about how to "build your network," I want you to throw that phrase out completely.

Don't build a network.

Weave a web of real relationships.

Relationships where you're not just asking, *What can they do for me?*

You're wondering, *How can I know them better? Support them better? Celebrate them better?*

Relationships where the goal isn't extraction - it's expansion.

You're not extracting favors or opportunities.

You're expanding possibility, for both of you.

It's a two-way street, built on the belief that **everyone has something valuable to offer, and everyone deserves to feel valued in return.**

And the beautiful thing about net-weaving?

It often starts with the smallest moves:

- A message that says, "Hey, I loved what you shared about your journey. Thanks for putting it out there."
- A handwritten note after a conference that says, "Meeting you was the highlight of my day."
- A comment on a post that goes deeper than "Congrats!" - that says, "I see the work and heart behind this. Well done."

Small, intentional acts.

Not because you want something.

Because you believe in connection as a value - not just a strategy.

And over time?

Those small moments weave a basket of trust, kindness, and mutual support that's stronger, more resilient, and far more fulfilling than anything you could manufacture through traditional networking tactics.

Practices You Can Start Today to Start Net-Weaving

Net-weaving isn't about grand gestures or complicated strategies.

It's built - strand by strand - in everyday interactions.

Here's what it looks like in practice:

1. Follow Up, Always.

If you meet someone - at a conference, in a training, on a plane - and you have a real conversation, follow up.

Not with a canned LinkedIn message that says, *"Let's connect!"*

With a *human* note.

Something like:

> *"I really enjoyed our conversation about leadership transitions. I'd love to stay in touch and hear how your next chapter unfolds."*

People remember when you circle back.

It tells them: *You weren't just polite in the moment. You cared enough to continue the thread.*

2. Remember the Details.

Like the story I wrote on the back of a business card about the woman with the aching feet and the new shoes.

Or the story of Amy, the fellow HR director on the plane, smiling and wondering if it was too early for a glass of wine.

These tiny details matter.

They anchor the connection in something real.

They tell the other person: *You mattered enough to remember.*

And when you reference those details later - in a message, a handwritten note, a catch-up conversation - it deepens trust instantly.

3. Share Opportunities Without Expectation.

One of the biggest ways to build real professional (and personal) webs of trust is this: **share without strings.**

If you see an article, a conference, a job opening, a scholarship, or a community event that reminds you of someone, send it to them.

No *"Hey, and by the way, could you do XYZ for me later?"*

Just, *"Saw this and thought of you."*

No agenda.

Just genuine care.

4. Move Beyond Professional Chit-Chat.

Sure, it's easy to ask, *"What do you do?"*

But net-weaving thrives when you ask deeper questions.

Like:

"What's lighting you up these days?"

"What's something you're passionate about outside of work?"

"Is there a cause or project you're excited about right now?"

These questions open doors that titles can't.

They invite people to show up as humans, not just profile or roles.

5. Show Up When It Matters Most.

Everyone loves connection when things are easy.

But trust is forged when things get hard.

When someone in your network shares a loss, a setback, a challenge - don't just like the post and scroll by.

Reach out.

- A short message: *"Thinking of you today."*
- A card in the mail: *"You're not alone."*
- An offer: *"If you want to grab coffee, I'm here."*

Presence in hard moments is worth more than a hundred endorsements on LinkedIn.

6. Be Willing to Go First.

Sometimes, especially in professional spaces, people are waiting for permission to be real.

Be the one who goes first.

- Share a story that's not polished.
- Admit when you're nervous.
- Celebrate a small, imperfect win.

Your vulnerability gives others permission to exhale and meet you there.

As researcher Dr. Julianne Holt-Lunstad from Brigham Young University found, **people are biologically wired to respond positively to emotional authenticity** [25].

When someone shows real emotion - whether it's joy, hope, fear, or uncertainty - it triggers empathy and strengthens connection.

In other words?

Your humanity is your greatest asset.

Not your perfection.

Not your polish.

Not your LinkedIn headline.

You.

Net-Weaving Is a Long Game - and It's Worth It

Here's the thing about building real, human-centered relationships:

It's not instant gratification.

You won't always see immediate "ROI."

You won't always land a big client or make a flashy connection five minutes after a coffee chat.

You might not even hear back every time you send a thoughtful note.

And that's okay.

Because net-weaving isn't about transactional gains.

It's about transformational trust.

It's about creating a web of relationships that sustains you - personally and professionally - over time.

The kind of web that catches you when you fall.

The kind of web that helps you rise when you're ready.

You don't have to chase everyone.

You don't have to force connection with people who aren't a fit.

You don't have to "collect" people like trophies on a shelf.

You just have to keep showing up with intention.

Keep noticing.

Keep reaching out.

Keep remembering the human behind the business card, the LinkedIn profile, the handshake.

Because one day, it won't be the person with the biggest network who thrives.

It'll be the person with the deepest one.

The person who nurtured real relationships when it wasn't convenient.

The one who stayed curious.

The one who kept weaving strand after strand, believing that trust and care matter more than any polished elevator pitch.

I'll leave you with this:

You have no idea whose life you might change by seeing them, remembering them, believing in them.

Sometimes a simple, unexpected note opens a door someone thought was closed.

Sometimes one conversation shifts the course of someone's career - or life.

Sometimes the moment you think is "too small to matter" is the one that matters most.

Not because you said the perfect thing.

Not because you followed some ten-step networking plan.

But because you showed up as yourself.

You stayed present.

You stayed human.

And in a world full of noise and performance?

That's the rarest, most powerful connection of all.

STOP Overthinking It

Pause. Reflect. Apply.

What to Remember

- Real professional (and personal) relationships aren't built through polished pitches - they're built through presence and care.
- Net-weaving is about layering connection strand-by-strand, like weaving a strong, flexible basket - not rushing to create a picture-perfect tapestry.
- Small, human moments often create the deepest, longest-lasting connections.
- LinkedIn, conferences, coffee chats - none of these require perfection. They require sincerity.
- You don't have to chase or impress everyone.
- You just have to show up fully with the people meant for you.

Self-Reflection

Take a few minutes to reflect - journal, think quietly, or talk it through with a trusted friend:

- Where am I focusing more on collecting contacts than nurturing real connections?
- When was the last time I slowed down and truly got curious about someone's story - without rushing to network?
- How do I feel when someone reaches out just because they value me - not because they need something?
- What simple act of follow-up (note, message, coffee invite) could I offer someone this week to deepen an existing relationship?
- Am I allowing space for connections to unfold naturally, or am I trying to control the outcome?

Try This Strategy

The Follow-Up Magic Rule

This week, after any new conversation - whether at a conference, a Zoom call, or even a casual meetup - take five minutes to do one simple thing:

- Send a quick message or handwritten note.
- Mention one small, real thing you noticed about them (*"I loved your story about how you got into this field"* / *"You made me laugh when you talked about your dog - thanks for that"*).
- No pitches. No asks. Just human follow-up.

It's a tiny practice that makes a massive difference over time - strand by strand, connection by connection.

Conversation Starter

Want to build more honest, warm connections without feeling like you're "networking"?

Try this the next time you meet someone:

"What's something you're excited about outside of work right now?"

You'll be amazed at how fast you move from small talk to real conversation - and how much richer your relationships will feel.

Chapter 10

Conversation is Connection

Better small talk. Deeper check-ins. Conflict without awkwardness.

If connection is the bridge between people, conversation is the way we build it - plank by plank, word by word.

But somewhere along the way, conversation started feeling… complicated.

We overthink what to say.

We dread awkward pauses.

We default to surface-level small talk and wonder why we leave feeling a little emptier, not fuller.

It's not because we're bad at talking.

It's because real connection asks for more than exchanging words — it asks for presence, curiosity, and courage.

And here's the truth:

You don't have to be dazzlingly witty, naturally extroverted, or masterfully polished to be a great conversationalist.

You just have to be willing to show up - real, open, and a little braver than usual.

Most of us were taught how to introduce ourselves, how to network, how to "work the room."

But few of us were taught how to create conversations that actually matter.

Conversations where people walk away feeling lighter, not heavier.

Where people feel more seen, not more evaluated.

That's what this chapter is about.

Not memorizing icebreakers.

Not perfecting your "elevator pitch."

But learning how conversation - even small, simple conversation - can become one of the greatest tools for building trust, belonging, and real connection in your life.

Let's start by debunking one of the biggest myths about meaningful conversation:

Small talk isn't the enemy.

A lot of connection advice out there loves to dunk on small talk.

You'll hear things like, *"Skip the small talk! Go deep immediately!"*

But the truth is, **small talk matters** - when you know how to use it.

Small talk, done with presence and intention, is like stretching before a long run.

It's not the point of the workout - but it warms you up.

It eases you in.

It gives both people a chance to find their footing, their pace, their energy.

Small talk isn't supposed to be life-changing.

It's supposed to be *life-opening.*

It's the casual "How's your day been so far?" that leads to discovering someone just got engaged.

It's the quick comment about the weather that opens up a conversation about someone's childhood in another part of the country.

It's the tiny, ordinary question that gently says, *"Hey, I'm safe. We can talk."*

In fact, research from the University of Chicago found that even brief conversations with strangers significantly boost happiness [26].

Small, genuine moments of interaction can actually create ripples of well-being - for you and for the people around you.

The key is presence.

Not polishing.

Not performing.

Just being there.

Brené Brown said it best when she wrote, *"Connection doesn't exist without giving people space to be seen and heard"* [27].

Small talk isn't about getting the other person to think you're smart or interesting.

It's about opening a door wide enough that a real conversation might one day walk through.

So instead of dismissing small talk as shallow, what if we reframed it as **setting the table for deeper connection?**

You don't expect a meal to magically appear on an empty table - you set the plates, pour the water, light the candle.

That's what small talk does.

It sets the conditions for trust to enter the room.

But here's where we often get stuck:

We overthink it.

We think we have to be brilliant.

Or profound.

Or hilarious.

We forget that the most powerful conversations usually start with something simple - and grow because someone was willing to stay a little longer, listen a little deeper, and ask a little more honestly.

If you've ever been trapped in your own head at a conference, standing awkwardly by the coffee station wondering how to start a conversation without sounding weird - you're not alone.

The secret?

Shift your focus.

Instead of trying to *be* interesting, focus on *being* interested.

Here are a few of my favorite low-pressure, high-connection starters:

"What's been the best part of your week so far?"

"Is this your first time at [event]?"

"I'm always looking for good [books/podcasts/restaurants]. Any recommendations?"

"What's something you're working on right now that you're excited about?"

Notice:

None of these demand brilliance.

None of them back someone into a yes/no corner.

They just invite realness.

They say: *You don't have to impress me. You just have to be you.*

And here's the beautiful part:

Most people are dying for someone to give them that kind of space.

Not space to perform.

Space to connect.

Beyond Small Talk: How to Have Deeper Check-Ins Without It Getting Awkward

Once you've opened the door with small talk, the next challenge is:

How do you step through it without making things weird?

Because let's be real - we've all had that moment where we try to go deeper and it just… lands flat.

The other person smiles politely.

Or gives a short answer.

Or visibly panics because they weren't expecting the conversation to suddenly feel like a therapy session.

Here's the key:

Depth doesn't have to mean heaviness.

It's not about prying into someone's private life five minutes after meeting them.

It's about creating space for realness to emerge naturally - without forcing it.

Think of it like tending a campfire:

You don't throw a giant log on right away.

You start with kindling.

You give it air.

You let the flames catch slowly.

The same goes for conversations.

Here's how to move beyond small talk without making it awkward:

1. **Offer a little first.**

Instead of jumping straight into deep questions, offer a small but real piece of yourself.

Example:

"Honestly, this week's been a little nuts - but I'm grateful to be here."

You're modeling vulnerability without oversharing.

You're giving permission: *It's safe to be real here.*

2. **Use "safe but real" questions.**

Instead of the standard *"What do you do?"* (which can feel transactional), try:

"What's something you're looking forward to?"

"What's been making you smile lately?"

"If you could magically add one extra hour to your day, what would you use it for?"

These questions aren't heavy.

But they invite depth.

They show you care about the *human*, not just the resume.

3. Watch for micro-signals.

If someone leans in, makes more eye contact, or shares something slightly more personal - that's an invitation.

It means they're willing to go a little deeper.

(But if they stay guarded or shift away, honor that too. Not everyone's ready, and that's okay.)

4. Normalize the lightness too.

Every conversation doesn't have to be life-altering.

Sometimes you'll plant seeds of trust that bloom later.

Sometimes a simple laugh or a shared observation builds just as much connection as a soul-baring moment.

Real connection doesn't come from forcing depth.

It comes from offering presence.

Handling Conflict Without Losing Connection

Here's the truth no one loves to admit:

If you're building real relationships, conflict isn't a maybe - it's a guarantee.

Disagreements, miscommunications, hurt feelings - they're part of the deal.

Not because anyone's doing anything wrong, but because connection involves real people.

And real people bring real differences.

The goal isn't to avoid conflict altogether.

(That's just performance and people-pleasing in disguise.)

The goal is to **move through conflict without burning the relationship down.**

Here's where overthinking loves to creep in:

- "Should I say something?"
- "What if I make it worse?"
- "Maybe I should just let it go…"
- "Am I being too sensitive?"

And suddenly, we're trapped - stuck between silent resentment and the fear of saying the wrong thing.

But what if conflict wasn't a threat to connection?

What if it was actually an opportunity to *deepen* it?

Healthy conflict is a trust builder, not a trust breaker.

(If you handle it with presence, not performance.)

Here's how:

1. Lead with curiosity, not accusation.

Instead of:

"You made me feel unimportant."

Try:

"When [X] happened, I felt a little unseen. Can we talk about it?"

Notice the shift?

You're sharing your experience, not labeling them.

2. **Stay connected to the person, not just the problem.**

It's easy to zero in on what went wrong.

It's harder - and more powerful - to stay connected to *why* the relationship matters.

Remind yourself (and sometimes even say out loud):

"I'm bringing this up because I value our connection, not because I want to fight."

3. **Focus on repair, not victory.**

You're not trying to win.

You're trying to understand.

You're trying to build something stronger than either of you could build alone.

4. **Normalize messy conversations.**

Conflict doesn't have to be clean and tidy to be productive.

It's okay if voices shake. It's okay if there's a pause while you both search for the right words.

What matters most is *staying* in it - not getting it perfect.

Presence during conflict says: *"You matter enough for me to stay."*

And when someone feels that?

Walls come down.

Real connection starts to grow roots.

Conversation is Connection (Even When It's Imperfect)

We overthink conversations all the time.

We rehearse. We edit. We predict.

We treat conversations like performances - like there's a "right" answer we're supposed to give.

But here's the quiet truth that frees you:

The goal of conversation isn't perfection.

It's connection.

It's not about crafting the most impressive statement.

It's about being real enough that someone else feels safe being real, too.

I've learned that people don't remember the exact words you said.

They remember how they *felt* talking to you:

- Did they feel heard?
- Did they feel respected?
- Did they feel valued?

That's the true success metric - not whether you sounded polished or brilliant.

In fact, research from MIT's Human Dynamics Lab found that the most successful teams didn't necessarily have the smartest people or the longest resumes.

They had the best communication patterns [28].

Specifically, teams that thrived showed:

- Equal participation in conversations (everyone's voice mattered)
- High levels of face-to-face communication
- Lots of back-and-forth, active listening

In other words:

Connection beats credentials.

Presence beats polish.

When we stop trying to "win" the conversation, we create space for it to *work*.

I saw this firsthand during a leadership retreat I was facilitating a leadership retreat a few years ago.

There was a senior leader - brilliant, experienced, the kind of person everyone looked up to - but whenever he spoke, the room went quiet.

Not because people were listening intently.

Because they were intimidated.

He spoke in full paragraphs, perfect phrasing, polished delivery.

It sounded impressive - but it didn't *feel* inviting.

Then, halfway through the second day, something shifted.

He raised his hand and, instead of offering another polished point, he said:

"I realize I've been talking at you more than with you. Truth is, I'm struggling with this change, too. I don't have all the answers."

The room exhaled.

You could *feel* the shift.

People leaned forward.

They started sharing.

They weren't performing anymore - they were participating.

All it took was one moment of honest, imperfect, human connection.

And it changed the tone of the entire retreat.

STOP OVERTHINKING IT

PAUSE. REFLECT. APPLY.

What to Remember

Small talk isn't small - it's the starting line for real connection.

Awkwardness is human. Presence, curiosity, and compassion are the antidotes.

Real conversations don't require perfect timing or flawless words - they require your heart.

You don't have to force depth. Trust builds naturally when you stay open and show up consistently.

A single sincere moment - a question, a story, a shared laugh - can shift the energy of a conversation, a meeting, or even a relationship.

People remember how you made them feel, not how polished your words were.

Self-Reflection

Take a few quiet minutes - no filter, no overthinking - and explore these questions:

- When do I feel most tempted to "perform" instead of simply connect?
- What's one situation recently where I wished a conversation had gone deeper? What held me back?
- Who in my life do I feel truly seen and relaxed with? What do they do differently in conversation?
- Where might I be overcomplicating connection - trying to script it instead of simply stepping into it?
- What would it look like to approach my next conversation as a chance to *connect*, not impress?

Try This Strategy

The "One Real Question" Rule

The next time you're in a conversation - whether it's a coffee chat, a team meeting, or a text thread - pause and ask yourself:

What's one real, human question I can ask that invites them to share more?

Examples:

"What's been the highlight of your week so far?"

"What's something you're excited about outside of work right now?"

"If you could wave a magic wand over your day, what would change?"

"What's something you're learning lately?"

You don't have to steer the conversation into profound depths every time -

you just have to open the door.

(And sometimes, the best conversations happen when you weren't trying to make them happen at all.)

Conversation Starter

Here's one you can use with a friend, a coworker, a client - anyone you want to build stronger connection with:

"What's something you wish people asked you about more often?"

You'll be amazed what you learn - and how much deeper the connection feels when you ask a question few others think to ask.

Chapter 11

Styles of Connection

How understanding yourself (and others) helps you stop overthinking relationships.

If you've ever walked away from a conversation replaying every word you said- or didn't say - you're not alone.

We overthink connection all the time.

"Did I come on too strong?"

"Did I say enough?"

"Why did they seem so distant?"

"Are they mad at me, or just busy?"

We swirl.

We second-guess.

We fill in gaps with stories about ourselves ("I'm too much," "I'm too boring") or about them ("They don't care," "They're mad at me").

But most of the time?

It's not a moral failure.

It's not rejection.

It's not a fatal flaw in your ability to connect.

It's just…different styles of connection.

We're wired differently.

We engage differently.

We express interest, care, affection, and trust differently.

And when we don't understand that - or when we assume everyone should show up like we do - we can start overthinking ourselves right out of the relationships we're trying to build.

Here's the good news:

When you understand that connection has different "styles" - like different languages people are speaking - everything gets easier.

You stop over-personalizing every delayed response.

You stop over-polishing every message.

You stop over-interpreting silence, short texts, or different energy levels.

You start seeing people for who they are - and accepting the beautiful, frustrating, human variety of connection that comes with that.

And maybe, most importantly:

You start accepting yourself, too.

Your way of connecting isn't wrong.

It's just one way.

One style in a big, rich, colorful range.

When you stop expecting every conversation to look the same - or every connection to move at the same pace - you free yourself to actually enjoy the messy, unpredictable, beautiful reality of human relationships.

And isn't that what we're really after?

Not a perfect script.

Not a flawless track record.

But real connection.

Connection that doesn't require you to micromanage every word or read every facial expression like a secret code.

Connection that feels like breathing, not performing.

That's what understanding styles of connection makes possible.

It doesn't mean you'll never feel awkward again.

It doesn't mean every conversation will be easy.

But it does mean you'll be equipped with a lot more grace - for yourself, and for everyone else you're trying to connect with.

And that's a game-changer.

Common Styles of Connection (and Why We Misread Each Other)

Let's get practical for a minute.

When you think about the way people connect, it's easy to assume there's a "right" way to do it:

Be warm. Be open. Be interested. Be consistent.

But here's the thing: "warm, open, interested, and consistent" look wildly different depending on the person.

Some people connect through energy and enthusiasm.

(Think: lots of emojis in texts, quick hugs, excited invitations.)

Others connect through steadiness and reliability.

(Think: showing up without fanfare, remembering the details you forgot you shared.)

Some connect through deep conversations.

(Think: late-night talks about dreams, fears, and big life questions.)

Some connect through shared activities.

(Think: "Let's go for a hike," or "Let's grab coffee and brainstorm together.")

Some people connect by giving practical help.

(Think: sending you a job posting they saw, fixing your flat tire, proofreading your résumé.)

Some connect by being present without words.

(Think: sitting quietly beside you when you're grieving, without needing to fill the silence.)

Here's where overthinking kicks in:

When someone connects differently than we do, we often assume they don't care.

We misread the signals because they don't look like the ones we're used to sending or receiving.

- The friend who doesn't text back right away? You might think they don't value you.
- The coworker who skips small talk and jumps into business? You might think they're cold.

- The boss who praises you quietly but never makes a big announcement? You might think they're not proud of you.
- The sibling who sends memes instead of deep emotional check-ins? You might think they're avoiding you.

But often, it's not a lack of care.

It's a difference in connection style.

When you realize that, you can stop filling in the blanks with worst-case assumptions.

You can start getting curious instead of critical.

You can meet people where they are, not where you wish they were.

And maybe even more important?

You can own your own style - and stop beating yourself up for not connecting "the way everyone else does."

Maybe you're the emoji-texting, heart-on-sleeve connector.

Maybe you're the steady presence who doesn't say much, but shows up without fail.

Maybe you're the deep-question-asker who doesn't care about the weather but cares deeply about someone's soul.

Whatever your style is - it's valid.

And the more you understand that connection can look (and feel) a lot of different ways,

the less you'll overthink every relationship you're trying to build.

You'll stop asking, "What's wrong with me?"

You'll stop asking, "What's wrong with them?"

And you'll start asking better, more generous questions:

"I wonder how they like to connect?"

"I wonder what feels natural for them?"

"I wonder how we can meet in the middle?"

Because real connection isn't about finding your carbon copy.

It's about building bridges between different hearts, different styles, different lives.

And that?

That's where the magic happens.

Stop Overthinking How You "Should" Connect (Start Noticing What Feels Real)

One of the biggest myths about connection is that some people are simply better at it - that it comes naturally, effortlessly, and without fear. But the truth? Connection isn't about natural charm. It's about presence. It's not about getting the words exactly right. It's about inviting someone into a space where they don't feel like they have to perform either.

When we overthink connection - when we obsess over whether we're saying the "right" thing, making the perfect impression, or sounding smart enough - we actually pull away from the very thing we're craving. We shift the focus inward: What do they think of me? Did I sound okay? Did I say too much?

And when that happens, we're not truly connecting.

We're managing.

We're performing.

We're trying to win belonging, rather than experiencing it.

Research backs this up: according to a study published in Personality and Social Psychology Bulletin, people who focused on managing impressions during conversations reported higher anxiety and lower feelings of authenticity and connection compared to those who focused simply on being present and curious [13]. In other words, the more we try to control how we're perceived, the less connected we actually feel.

Connection isn't something you engineer perfectly - it's something you enter imperfectly.

It's in the text you almost overthought but sent anyway:

"Thought of you today. Hope you're doing okay."

It's in the awkward laugh that bubbles up during a conversation and reminds you both that you're just human.

It's in the simple, sincere moments when you say:

"I'm not sure what the right words are here, but I'm really glad we're talking."

You don't need to strategize your way into deeper relationships.

You just need to stay open enough to be real.

Because connection isn't built when we impress someone.

It's built when we invite someone.

Invite them to feel seen.

Invite them to feel safe.

Invite them to be human alongside you.

And the secret most people don't realize?

They're craving that permission just as much as you are.

In a world that rewards polish, perfection, and curated highlight reels, offering presence - messy, wholehearted, unpolished presence - is an act of generosity. It's a reminder that they don't have to overthink it either. They just have to show up.

And together? That's where real connection begins.

STOP Overthinking It

Pause. Reflect. Apply.

What to Remember

- Connection isn't about getting it right. It's about staying real.
- Overthinking how you're coming across actually shrinks connection, not strengthens it.
- People aren't looking for perfect conversations; they're looking for sincere presence.
- Managing impressions increases anxiety. Choosing presence builds trust.
- The more you allow yourself to be human, the more you invite others to be human too.

Self-Reflection

- Take a few minutes to sit with these questions. You don't have to answer all of them at once - just pick one or two that tug at you:
- Where in my life do I most overthink how I'm coming across?
- When was the last time I felt deeply connected with someone? What made that moment feel safe and real?
- What would change if I focused less on "getting it right" and more on being fully present?
- What assumptions am I making about what people expect from me—and are they even true?
- What if connection didn't have to be earned, but simply allowed?

Try This Strategy

The 70% Rule

(Adapted from emotional intelligence research on authentic communication)

Next time you catch yourself trying to "perfect" a conversation or networking moment, try this:

1. If what you're about to say feels about 70% ready, go ahead and say it.
2. Don't wait until your words are 100% polished, packaged, and perfect.
3. Trust that presence matters more than precision.

Most meaningful conversations aren't 100% polished. They're 70% thought-out, 30% heart-on-sleeve.

That's what makes them feel alive.

Conversation Starter

Want to practice low-pressure connection without overthinking it?

Next time you're with someone (a friend, colleague, even a new acquaintance), try asking:

"What's something small that's been bringing you joy lately?"

It's simple.

It's real.

And it opens the door to human connection without the pressure of having the "perfect" deep talk.

PART IV
Beyond the First Step

Chapter 12

From "Hi" to Trust

What deepens relationships over time and how to nurture them.

It's one thing to make a connection.

It's another thing entirely to build a relationship that lasts.

We live in a world of quick hits: a follow on Instagram, a "like" on LinkedIn, a handshake at a conference. These are important starts - but real trust, the kind that makes professional relationships thrive and personal bonds deepen, doesn't happen at the starting line.

It happens in the middle.

In the quiet.

In the spaces between the big moments.

When you think about the people you trust most - the ones you'd call when life hits the fan - chances are it wasn't one dazzling first impression that cemented that relationship.

It was the small, consistent ways they showed up over time.

Consistency builds trust.

Curiosity keeps it growing.

Care keeps it alive.

And if you're like most people, you overthink this part more than you realize.

You worry:

- Am I following up too much?
- Not enough?
- Am I annoying them?
- Did I say the wrong thing?
- Are they pulling back because they're busy - or because I said something weird?

You start to assume. You start to shrink. You start to second-guess.

And often, you pull back just when the relationship is at the brink of deepening.

This is the silent heartbreak of overthinking relationships: we bail out too soon.

Not because the connection wasn't real, but because we didn't trust ourselves enough to stay in it long enough.

The good news?

We can break that pattern.

We can nurture relationships the same way we started them - with presence, curiosity, and courage.

Because trust isn't built in grand moments. It's layered, slowly, through consistent, genuine interaction over time.

It's in the everyday moments when you show up - without agenda, without pretense, without needing it to be perfect.

It's the small follow-up after someone shares a challenge:

> *"Hey, I was thinking about what you said yesterday - how are you feeling today?"*

It's the remembering of details that seem minor but aren't: the name of their dog, the big presentation they were preparing for, the city their mom just moved to.

These micro-moments don't feel glamorous or impressive in the moment.

They're easy to overlook. Easy to postpone.

But they're the ones that matter most.

Because every time you show someone they're remembered, every time you extend a simple, thoughtful thread between you, you stitch another layer into the relationship.

And no, it doesn't have to be constant.

It doesn't mean you need to schedule regular check-ins or manage relationships like a project plan.

It simply means adopting a mindset of staying open, staying present, and staying willing - willing to reach, to notice, to care, even imperfectly.

Because it's not about frequency.

It's about presence.

The way you show up - even sporadically - can leave a bigger imprint than daily conversations that stay on the surface.

And when in doubt? Assume people are glad to be remembered.

Very few people think, "Ugh, why did they reach out?"

Most think, "Wow, that was kind." Even if they never say it aloud.

And here's another truth that overthinking tries to hide from us:

Trust deepens in imperfection.

Not in the moments when we get everything right.

Not when we always have the perfect response or the seamless follow-up.

But when we risk showing up imperfectly - and still show up anyway.

It's reaching out even if it's been a while and you're worried they might be upset.

It's admitting, *"I meant to check in sooner, but you've been on my mind."*

It's sending the message even if you fumble the words a little.

Because when someone sees that you cared enough to reach out - despite your fear of it being awkward, despite the imperfection - it builds something stronger than polished communication ever could.

It builds emotional safety.

It builds belonging.

It builds a sense that you're not just connected when everything's easy - you're connected even when it's messy.

Dr. Brené Brown talks about how connection requires courage: the courage to be vulnerable, to reach out without a guaranteed outcome, to risk feeling a little exposed [27].

And this is especially true in the spaces between first meetings and deep trust.

Because trust isn't a switch.

It's a garden.

And every small moment of real presence is another seed planted.

Sometimes you'll see it grow right away - a text back, a returned smile, a grateful hug.

Sometimes it feels like nothing happened.

But the seed is there.

And trust me, the people who are meant to be part of your circle?

They notice.

They remember.

They feel it.

Not because you said it perfectly.

But because you cared enough to stay in the relationship - even in the quiet spaces where nothing big was happening.

And when you stay long enough in any real relationship - professional, personal, friendship - you're going to hit some bumps.

Misunderstandings. Missed expectations. Small hurts that fester if they aren't addressed.

And this is where a lot of relationships plateau - or quietly start to fade.

Because if we overthink those moments, we often make them bigger than they are:

> "They didn't text back - they must not care about me."
>
> "I said something awkward - maybe I ruined it."
>
> "We haven't talked in a while - it's probably too late to reach out."

So instead of reaching out, we retreat.

Instead of repairing, we withdraw.

And a thread that could have been mended… breaks instead.

But if we practice staying present even in the awkwardness - if we dare to believe that one imperfect moment doesn't erase everything good - we open the door to deeper trust.

Because real trust isn't built by never making mistakes.

It's built by how we show up after the mistake.

Repair is one of the most powerful trust builders we have.

It says: "This relationship matters more to me than my pride. More than my ego. More than being 'right.'"

And research backs this up. Dr. Gottman's studies found that the success of relationships isn't about avoiding conflict - it's about the ability to repair after conflict [10].

The relationships that thrive aren't the ones with perfect communication.

They're the ones where people make small course corrections along the way.

Where someone says, *"Hey, that didn't land the way I intended. Can we talk about it?"*

Where someone sends the *"Hey, I miss you"* text even when it feels vulnerable.

Where silence isn't automatically assumed to mean rejection.

It's not about being flawless.

It's about being faithful to the connection - especially when it's tested.

Every time we risk reaching out after a misstep - every time we choose curiosity over assumptions, care over defensiveness - we're laying down another stone in the foundation of trust.

And it doesn't have to be dramatic.

Sometimes it sounds like:

"Hey, I realized I might have seemed distracted during our conversation yesterday. I'm sorry. You matter to me."

Or:

"I miss hearing what's going on with you. Life got hectic, but I want to reconnect if you're open to it."

Or simply:

"I think I misunderstood you earlier. Can we revisit that?"

Small. Honest. Human.

These tiny repair attempts signal something vital:

I value you enough to stay.

I trust this relationship enough to be awkward if it means being honest.

And over time, these moments - just like Gottman's "small trust moments" [10] - accumulate into something sturdy.

Something that can weather harder conversations.

Something that can withstand distance, mistakes, busy seasons, misunderstandings.

Because trust isn't a feeling you have once and then check off the list.

Trust is a living, breathing thing.

It's built - and rebuilt - every day, in the choices we make to stay engaged.

Especially when it would be easier to pull away.

Especially when it feels scary to reach out first.

Especially when our own overthinking tries to convince us it's not worth it.

When you feel that pull to retreat - pause.

Ask yourself: What matters more here: my fear of looking foolish, or the connection I actually want to build?

Choosing connection over comfort is hard.

But it's the difference between surface relationships and lasting ones.

Connection Isn't Built in the Highlight Reel

One of the biggest lies we tell ourselves - especially in professional spaces - is that relationships are built through "big moments."

The perfect LinkedIn post that goes viral.

The flawless presentation that wins over the room.

The impressive bio shared before you step on stage.

But the truth?

People might admire your highlights.

They trust your humanity.

Real connection deepens in the in-between spaces - the casual check-ins, the "thinking of you" texts, the moments where you show up not because it's strategic, but because it's real.

A 2022 study published in the Journal of Social and Personal Relationships found that the frequency and quality of everyday interactions were a stronger predictor of relational closeness than major life events [13].

Translation:

It's not the conference keynote or the big award ceremony that forges bonds.

It's the DM you send congratulating a colleague without expecting anything back.

It's the coffee you grab together just because you genuinely like hearing about their messy, real life.

It's the way you circle back three weeks later to ask, *"Hey, how did that big client meeting go?"*

When we only show up for people's highlight moments - or when we only let others see ours - we're missing the depth that comes from being there for the messy, uncurated middle.

If connection were a fire, it wouldn't be built with fireworks.

It would be built with steady kindling: small twigs, everyday sparks, patient tending.

And the beautiful part?

You don't have to be the most charismatic person in the room to build that kind of trust.

You just have to be someone who stays present through the ordinary moments.

The ones that don't make it onto anyone's feed.

The ones that don't look impressive from the outside.

The ones that whisper, I see you. I care. I'm still here.

Because in the end, it's not the highlight reel that builds relationships.

It's the real reel.

The one you don't curate.

The one you live.

Presence Over Performance, Revisited

It's worth repeating: people don't build lasting trust based on your résumé, your wit, or your perfectly crafted small talk.

They build it based on your presence over time.

Dr. Amy Edmondson, the Harvard researcher behind the concept of psychological safety, emphasizes that consistent, genuine engagement - especially in small, informal moments - creates environments where trust naturally flourishes [29].

The same is true outside of teams. In personal relationships, micro-moments of presence weave the fabric of trust much more tightly than grand gestures ever could.

The hard part?

Staying consistent when life gets busy.

When work piles up.

When you start overthinking, Have I reached out too much? Not enough? Will it seem weird if I send another text?

This is where people accidentally distance themselves without meaning to.

They pull back, thinking they're protecting the relationship ("I don't want to bother them") - when really, they're withholding the very thing that deepens it: real presence.

When you feel that hesitation rising - that internal debate about whether it's "weird" to follow up, check in, or simply say "I'm thinking of you" - remember:

Trust doesn't grow from perfection.

It grows from genuine, imperfect presence.

(And often, the person you're second-guessing reaching out to? They're hoping you will.)

The Invisible Thread: Why Trust Isn't About Big Moments

We tend to believe that trust is earned through grand displays - a huge favor, a major sacrifice, a dramatic "I'll be there for you no matter what" moment.

And sure, big moments matter.

But research consistently shows that trust is actually built (and broken) in the smallest interactions.

The Gottman Institute refers to this phenomenon as the "trust metric" [30].

It's not one massive act of loyalty that makes someone trust you - it's the repeated, ordinary signals that say:

- "You matter to me, even when there's nothing in it for me."
- "I'm paying attention, even when life is busy."
- "I'm still here, even when things get messy."

Think about the relationships in your life you trust most deeply.

It's probably not because someone once showed up big for you (although that's beautiful when it happens).

It's because they kept showing up - in the small, unnoticed ways - long after the initial spark, long after it would have been easy to drift apart.

It's not magic.

It's muscle.

Trust is a muscle we build one small, real interaction at a time.

When we overthink connection, we put enormous pressure on ourselves to "make an impression," "say the perfect thing," or "create a moment" that seals the bond.

But trust doesn't demand that kind of performance.

It asks for something much simpler - and much harder:

- Consistency over intensity.
- Genuine attention over polished effort.
- Curiosity over control.

Instead of worrying about how to "network better" or "impress someone important," the real magic happens in the small, quiet choices we make again and again.

The text you send even when you're not sure what to say.

The quick "thinking of you" message after a tough week.

The way you keep showing up when there's nothing flashy to gain - just the slow weaving of trust, strand by imperfect strand.

The truth is, trust doesn't need grand gestures.

It needs human ones.

And the beautiful part?

When you stop trying to manufacture trust, and simply start building it through presence, everything gets lighter.

You don't have to analyze every interaction afterward.

You don't have to script out the next conversation in your head.

You don't have to overthink your worth based on whether someone replied to your last message in 30 minutes or three days.

You anchor your confidence somewhere deeper:

in knowing that trust is a long game,

in trusting yourself to show up real,

in believing that small, steady gestures matter more than grand impressions.

This shift changes how you approach everything:

- Networking becomes net-weaving - slow, meaningful, and human.
- Follow-up becomes relationship-building - not sales pitches or favor trades.
- First impressions become first invitations - to real connection, not performance.

When you stop trying to "win" people and start choosing to see them - really see them - you become the kind of person others trust naturally.

Not because you said the perfect thing.

Not because you impressed them.

But because you stayed.

Because you cared enough to show up without a script.

Because you made connection feel safe, easy, and human.

So what does this actually look like in real life?

It looks like replying to someone's good news with more than just "Congrats!" - but actually asking, *"How did it feel when you found out?"*

It looks like remembering someone's birthday without needing a Facebook reminder - and sending a message that's personal, not perfunctory.

It looks like checking in a month after someone mentions they're struggling — not just the day after.

It looks like following up when you say, *"Let's grab coffee sometime,"* and actually scheduling it.

It looks like sending the article, the podcast, the funny meme - not because you're trying to "stay top of mind," but because you genuinely thought of them and wanted to brighten their day.

These are the things people remember.

Not the perfectly worded email.

Not the business card exchange.

Not the LinkedIn endorsement.

It's the quiet, steady, unspectacular moments that say:

"You matter to me, even when it's not convenient, even when it's not public, even when there's nothing in it for me."

That's how trust deepens.

Not all at once.

Not with a grand gesture.

But moment by moment, choice by choice, in the soft spaces where nobody's keeping score.

Sometimes, we don't even realize trust is building until we feel it.

It's in the way a conversation gets a little easier.

The way a silence between you isn't uncomfortable anymore.

The way you start being a little more yourself - not calculating every word, not double-checking every text.

Here are a few signs trust is quietly growing:

- Laughter comes more easily. You don't feel the need to perform or impress - you can simply enjoy each other's company.
- People bring you their small, real stories. Not just the polished wins, but the messy middles: the job stress, the parenting struggles, the doubt they usually keep tucked away.
- The follow-up feels natural. You don't have to script the next conversation or overthink if you're being "too much." You want to stay in touch - and so do they.
- You start to relax into who you are. You're not constantly second-guessing if you're being "professional enough" or "interesting enough." You just…are.

Trust isn't loud.

It doesn't make a big entrance.

It tiptoes in, quiet and steady, layering comfort over caution until connection feels safe.

And here's the thing:

If you're always waiting for someone else to prove they're trustworthy before you risk showing up real, you might be waiting a long time.

Sometimes you have to go first.

You have to offer a little softness before you're sure how it'll be received.

You have to extend trust, not because you're naïve, but because you're brave.

Trust grows when we choose presence over performance - again and again.

Not perfectly. Not fearlessly. But intentionally.

Overthinking erodes trust.

If presence builds trust, overthinking slowly chips away at it.

It doesn't happen because we're careless or cruel.

It happens because when we're stuck in our heads - analyzing every word, replaying every conversation, crafting the "perfect" response - we're not really present anymore.

We become harder to read.

Harder to trust.

Harder to feel connected to.

Because overthinking creates distance.

Think about the last time you were with someone who seemed distracted - not in a malicious way, but because they were clearly spinning in their own mind.

Maybe you were telling them a story, and you could see the moment they drifted.

Their eyes darted. Their smile tightened. Their attention fractured.

You didn't feel rejected - but you didn't feel held, either.

That's what overthinking does.

It subtly sends the message:

"I'm not fully here."

"I'm not fully with you."

"I'm too busy managing my own inner narrative to meet you in this moment."

And even if you didn't intend it, the impact is the same: trust doesn't deepen.

It stalls.

It hesitates.

It stays shallow when it could have gone deeper.

Presence says, "You matter."

Overthinking says, "I'm not sure if I'm enough."

And people can feel the difference - even if they don't consciously know what they're feeling.

The good news?

You don't have to eliminate overthinking completely to build trust. (Spoiler: nobody can.)

You just have to notice when you're slipping into performance mode - and gently guide yourself back to presence.

You can pause.

You can breathe.

You can say, *"I'm overthinking - let me just be here."*

And every time you do, you're strengthening the foundation of trust, one imperfect, human moment at a time.

Consistency Compounds

Trust doesn't hinge on sweeping gestures or singular breakthroughs.

It's built through small, repeated acts of care.

It's sending a quick text when you think of someone - not a perfect, polished message - just, "Hey, you crossed my mind. Hope you're doing okay."

It's remembering something that matters to them - their dog's surgery, their mom's recovery, their big work project - and following up weeks later.

It's saying, *"I don't have the right words, but I'm here"* when someone's hurting.

Each moment on its own might feel tiny. Insignificant, even.

But together?

They add up.

They create a steady hum of reliability:

"I can count on you."

"You show up."

"You see me even when there's nothing big happening."

That's what builds unshakable trust - not grand declarations, but small consistencies layered over time.

And here's something the research backs up:

Psychologist and best-selling author Dr. Sue Johnson, known for her work on emotional bonding, explains that trust is an emotional bond reinforced by responsiveness [31].

Responsiveness means we notice each other's emotional cues - and we respond.

Not perfectly.

Not always immediately.

But consistently enough that the other person's nervous system learns, "It's safe to lean toward you."

That's what turns "nice to meet you" into "I trust you."

It's a slow building, not a sudden leap.

It's quiet loyalty, not flashy loyalty.

It's hundreds of small repairs when life inevitably gets messy - not a perfect record of never messing up.

If you want deeper relationships, you don't need a genius-level conversation starter or a 10-point follow-up plan.

You need to keep showing up, in small, thoughtful ways, again and again.

You don't have to be perfect.

You just have to be present often enough that it starts to feel safe.

The Slow Fade of Disconnection

Just as trust builds slowly through consistent presence, disconnection doesn't usually happen overnight either.

It creeps in quietly.

It's the unanswered text that you mean to reply to… but don't.

The coffee catch-up you keep rescheduling.

The birthday you forget.

The message you see, but don't acknowledge because you're "too busy."

None of these alone break a relationship.

But over time?

They create tiny gaps.

Gaps that widen if we're not careful.

And here's the dangerous part: our brain fills in those gaps with stories.

Stories like:

> *"They don't care."*
>
> *"I'm not that important to them."*
>
> *"I'm always the one reaching out."*

It's not the missed lunch date that fractures trust.

It's the silence afterward.

It's the lack of repair.

Connection isn't maintained by perfection.

It's maintained by repair.

Research from Dr. Edward Tronick's "Still Face Experiment" [32] showed that even infants experience stress when a caregiver is unresponsive - but the relationship repairs and even strengthens when the caregiver re-engages warmly.

In other words: you don't have to be flawlessly connected all the time.

You just have to notice when disconnection happens - and turn back toward the person.

That's powerful news.

It means you can catch the small moments of drift before they become canyons.

You can send a quick, *"Hey, I know I've been MIA - thinking of you"* text.

You can admit, *"I dropped the ball. I'm sorry."*

You can say, *"I miss our conversations. Can we reconnect?"*

Simple. Human. Repair.

The people who stay deeply connected aren't the ones who never mess up.

They're the ones who notice the drift early - and turn back toward each other.

How to Nurture Trust Over Time

If trust grows in the middle, and if drift is inevitable sometimes, then how do we actually stay close?

It's not by tightening our grip on people.

It's not by micromanaging every interaction.

It's by tending to the relationship the way you would tend to a living thing - a plant, a garden, a child, a dream.

You water it.

You check in on it.

You notice when it looks a little droopy and needs extra care.

You adjust when the seasons shift.

Relationships are alive.

And like anything alive, they need different things at different times.

Here are a few truths that help me nurture trust over time - truths I've seen play out in friendships, family, mentorships, work teams, and partnerships:

Consistency matters more than intensity.

You don't have to blow people away with grand gestures.

You just have to show up with small, genuine presence consistently.

(Think tiny stitches that eventually make the quilt.)

Listening is action.

Sometimes we think we need to do something to prove we care.

But often, just listening - without fixing, without rushing - is what deepens trust.

Listening says: "You matter. Your experience matters. I'm not here to manage you; I'm here with you."

Vulnerability builds bridges.

When you let someone see you - the real you, not the polished one - it invites them to bring more of themselves, too.

Trust doesn't deepen through perfection. It deepens through "me too" moments.

Mismatch moments aren't fatal - unless ignored.

You will have moments where you misread each other.

Moments where you disappoint, frustrate, or even hurt each other.

That doesn't mean the connection is broken - it means you're human.

Acknowledgment and repair are the secret ingredients.

Don't wait until it's "the perfect time."

Connection isn't about a flawless calendar invite.

It's the random, quick texts.

The voice memos on a walk.

The silly memes sent after a long day.

The "thinking of you" note when you're not sure what to say.

(There is no perfect time. Now is good enough.)

The Power of Relational Deposits

Think of trust like a bank account.

Every time you show up with care, listen without judgment, celebrate someone's win, or simply remember a small detail about their life - you make a deposit.

Every time you miss a bid for connection, dismiss someone's feelings, fail to follow through, or only reach out when you need something - you make a withdrawal.

One moment doesn't make or break a relationship.

It's the pattern over time that either builds a solid balance… or leaves the account dangerously low.

Tiny acts of attention build massive reserves.

Remembering their favorite coffee order.

Checking in before a big meeting.

Noticing when their energy is different and gently asking if they're okay.

These aren't grand gestures. But they compound.

Withdrawals happen - and that's normal.

You're going to forget things.

You're going to have days when you're distracted or overwhelmed.

The goal isn't to never make a withdrawal - it's to notice when you do, and make a repair.

("Hey, I realized I was really short with you yesterday. I'm sorry. You didn't deserve that.")

You can't automate connection.

You can't schedule a quarterly coffee and assume trust will deepen.

Relationships breathe.

They need organic check-ins, not just calendar invites.

(One of the biggest mistakes leaders make is thinking a once-a-year retreat replaces daily care.)

In short:

You don't build trust by waiting until you have time to "do it right."

You build trust by doing something real - now!

Even a quick voice note:

> *"Hey, just thinking about you today. Hope your week is going okay."*

Even a random text - (my friend Julianne is REALLY good at this):

> *"Saw this and it made me smile - thought of you."*

Even a quiet check-in:

> *"I noticed you seemed a little off this morning. Just wanted to say I'm here if you want to talk."*

None of these take more than a minute.

But each one leaves a fingerprint.

A message that says: "You're not invisible. You matter to me."

How to Rebuild When Trust Gets Shaky

Even with the best intentions, every relationship will face bumps.

It's inevitable.

We miss a text we meant to answer.

We cancel plans last-minute because life overwhelmed us.

We say something thoughtless without realizing how deeply it cut.

It's easy to slip into overthinking at that point - replaying the mistake, agonizing over the perfect way to fix it, fearing we've caused irreparable harm. But here's the truth: trust isn't built on perfection. It's built on repair.

In her groundbreaking work on trust and vulnerability, Dr. Brené Brown reminds us that trust is a product of small moments over time [27] - and that includes how we navigate mistakes. The strongest relationships aren't the ones that never falter. They're the ones where repair is possible, welcomed, and handled with care.

When a crack forms in trust, the worst thing we can do is disappear into shame or defensiveness. It's tempting to either pretend it didn't happen ("It wasn't that big of a deal...") or spiral into self-judgment ("I'm terrible at relationships..."). Neither of these reactions helps us rebuild.

What does help?

Presence.

Accountability.

Careful, intentional reconnection.

Here's what that actually looks like:

First, own it early. You don't have to deliver a perfect apology. You don't have to draft a three-page letter of remorse. But you do have to acknowledge the impact of your actions - or your absence. A simple, sincere opening matters:

"I realize I haven't been as present lately. I'm sorry if that made you feel unimportant. It wasn't my intention, and you matter to me."

Notice the difference: you're not defending yourself ("I've just been busy!") or minimizing the hurt ("You're being too sensitive."). You're honoring the experience of the other person - without trying to make yourself the hero or the villain.

And then, the harder part: stay present.

Stay for the uncomfortable silence.

Stay for the reaction you can't control.

Stay for the real conversation that might follow.

You don't have to fix everything in a single moment. You just have to remain open enough to let healing start.

Emerging research from Stanford's Graduate School of Business emphasizes that repairing and enhancing trust requires more than just a quick apology - it takes deliberate, sustained effort. In a comprehensive review, Dr. Roderick Kramer and colleagues explored how trust, once damaged, can be restored through transparency, consistency, and proactive relationship-building. Their findings show that trust durability is not about avoiding mistakes altogether, but about how intentionally we respond when they happen. Meaningful repair - especially when paired with ongoing follow-through - can be more influential in strengthening relationships than avoiding conflict in the first place [33].

And it's not about grand gestures.

It's the small, consistent things:

- A sincere "I'm sorry" without rushing to justify.
- A text that says "I'm thinking of you" without expecting a response.
- An invitation to reconnect without pressure or guilt.
- A willingness to listen more than you speak.

Repair is an act of courage. It requires you to be brave enough to admit that you are human - that you sometimes miss, mess up, or fall short. And it requires you to trust that the relationship is strong enough to hold that truth.

Because real trust isn't built on the illusion that we'll never hurt each other.

It's built on the commitment to come back after we do.

Repair is a Process, Not a Performance

Real repair isn't about crafting the perfect apology.

It's about building a bridge - one small, honest plank at a time.

It might sound like:

"I realize I misunderstood what you needed. Can we talk about it?"

"I hate that what I said hurt you. That wasn't my intent - and I want to understand."

"I noticed things felt a little off after our last conversation. I care about this and want to clear the air."

Notice: none of these are elaborate.

None of them require grand speeches.

They just require humility, awareness, and the willingness to stay.

Because trust isn't about avoiding mistakes.

It's about what you do after the mistake.

And the biggest thing most people underestimate?

Timing matters.

In the Stanford research, one of the strongest predictors of relational recovery wasn't how perfectly someone apologized - it was how quickly they attempted to repair [33].

Waiting too long sends a different message: avoidance, indifference, pride.

But even a messy, imperfect repair - done sooner rather than later - communicates: you matter more than my comfort.

That's powerful.

And here's something even bigger:

Sometimes the true "repair" isn't what you say - it's what you consistently do afterward.

If you've broken trust by showing up late? Show up early.

If you missed an emotional cue? Slow down next time and ask.

If you said something careless? Be more mindful in the future - and let them see the shift.

Because real repair is visible.

It's embodied, not just explained.

The First Repair Is With Yourself

Before we can truly repair with others, we often have to start by repairing with ourselves.

Because when something goes wrong - a conversation falls apart, a friendship drifts, a moment gets misunderstood - it's easy to default to self-blame:

"I'm terrible at relationships."

"I always mess things up."

"Maybe I'm just too much (or not enough)."

That shame spiral doesn't make us better at connection.

It makes us smaller.

It convinces us that it's safer to stay distant, silent, unseen.

But if you want to build real trust with others, you have to rebuild trust with yourself first.

That begins by interrupting the shame story with something softer:

"I'm a human who cares - and sometimes caring gets messy."

"I'm willing to learn, even if I don't always get it right the first time."

"Mistakes don't erase my worth. They're invitations to grow."

Self-repair is the practice of offering yourself the same grace you're trying to offer others.

Because the truth is, you can't give from an empty well.

If you're carrying self-contempt, your attempts at external repair will feel forced - brittle, anxious, transactional.

But if you approach yourself with compassion, you approach others with true presence.

Repair starts inside.

And the more you practice it there, the more natural it becomes everywhere else. Keep in mind that when repair feels awkward, that's actually a good sign.

Let's be honest: repairing a relationship - even in small ways - almost never feels "smooth" at first.

It feels clumsy.

It feels exposed.

It feels like walking into a room where you're not sure if you're still welcome.

And that's normal.

If you're feeling awkward, it's not because you're doing it wrong.

It's because you're doing something brave.

The discomfort of repair is a sign that you're moving toward connection, not away from it. It's emotional growing pains - the tension between wanting to stay safe and wanting to stay close.

In fact, research from the Stanford Social Neuroscience Lab suggests that vulnerability-based actions (like repair attempts) activate the same neural pathways associated with physical risk [34].

Your brain is literally reading emotional openness as a form of risk-taking.

But here's the good news:

- Courage grows every time you lean in.
- Awkwardness fades faster than regret.
- And real connection almost always lives on the other side of that awkwardness.

If you wait to repair until it feels comfortable, you'll wait forever.

Instead, get good at moving through the awkwardness on purpose:

- Start small. A simple "Hey, can we check in?" can be enough.
- Own your part without over-explaining or self-shaming.
- Focus on how the relationship feels, not just what happened.
- Stay curious about their perspective - not defensive.

You don't have to say it perfectly.

You just have to stay present.

The goal isn't a flawless apology.

It's a restored bridge.

What Real-Life Repair Can Actually Sound Like

When you're ready to repair - whether after a misunderstanding, a missed moment, or an emotional stumble - it helps to have simple, honest language at your fingertips.

Here are a few examples of what real repair sounds like (no dramatic speeches or perfect phrasing required):

"I realize I wasn't fully present earlier, and I'm sorry. You matter to me. Can we start over?"

"I think I misunderstood you, and I jumped to conclusions. I'm sorry about that. I want to understand better."

"I felt defensive and shut down - not because of you, but because of my own stuff. I'm working on it. Thanks for your patience."

"I said that poorly. What I meant to say was that I value what you bring - and I want to keep hearing your thoughts."

"I know I hurt you. And while I can't undo it, I want you to know I see it, I care, and I'm here to rebuild trust if you're willing."

Notice what's missing?

No:

Grand justifications

Shiny explanations

Performative over-apologies

Just honest presence.

Real repair isn't about making yourself look good.

It's about making the relationship stronger.

It's about saying, in essence:

"You matter more to me than my pride.

You matter more to me than my need to be 'right.'

You matter more to me than my fear of being vulnerable."

And here's a powerful truth:

The willingness to repair - even imperfectly - is often more healing than the original hurt was damaging.

People don't need you to be flawless.

They need to know you care enough to keep choosing them - even when it's messy.

But here's the part we often miss about repair:

It's not just about saying the right words.

It's about being willing to stay - even if the outcome isn't immediate, clean, or comfortable.

A lot of us rush the repair moment without realizing it.

We say "I'm sorry" quickly, hoping for an instant "It's okay" in return.

We patch over the hurt like putting a Band-Aid on a deeper wound, hoping if we smile and move on fast enough, it'll all disappear.

But real repair doesn't happen on demand.

It happens when we create enough emotional space for trust to breathe again.

That means:

- Giving the other person room to feel whatever they feel.
- Being willing to sit in the discomfort if they're not ready to move forward yet.
- Resisting the urge to overexplain, overjustify, or pressure them to reassure you.

Because when we rush repair, we're not actually connecting.

We're managing our own anxiety.

And relationships aren't built on managing appearances.

They're built on honoring experiences - even when they're messy.

It might sound like:

"Take whatever time you need. I'm here."

"I don't expect you to be okay right away. I just want you to know I care."

"Even if you're not ready to talk yet, I'm not going anywhere."

Those are the moments that build something bigger than comfort.

They build trust.

And trust - real trust - isn't built by speeding through the hard parts.

It's built by being willing to stay for them.

The real beauty of slow, steady repair is that it doesn't just heal the current hurt.

It rewires the relationship for resilience.

Every time you stay when it would be easier to retreat, you send a message far louder than any apology could ever deliver:

You're safe with me - even when things are hard.

And over time, that message creates something rare.

Not just a connection that feels good when everything's easy - but a connection that holds when life gets heavy, when misunderstandings happen, when the inevitable messiness of being human shows up.

That's the kind of relationship most people are starving for.

Not a perfect one.

Not a pain-free one.

But a real one.

A relationship where bumps aren't deal-breakers, where disagreements aren't exits, where mistakes aren't silent severances.

Because here's the truth that's easy to forget in the heat of the moment:

Most relationships don't break because of one fight, one misstep, one bad day.

They break because, when the cracks appear, no one stays long enough to heal them.

But you can be different.

You can stay.

You can be the one who chooses care over closure.

Connection over correctness.

Curiosity over conclusions.

You can breathe through the discomfort.

You can listen when your ego wants to defend.

You can stay soft when the world tells you to harden.

And little by little - tiny moment by tiny moment - you can build something real.

Something strong.

Something that won't crumble the first time it's tested.

Because the goal isn't to never have cracks.

The goal is to become the kind of person who knows how to heal them.

STOP OVERTHINKING IT

PAUSE. REFLECT. APPLY.

What to Remember

1. Repair isn't about grand apologies - it's about small, honest moments of showing up.
2. Conflict doesn't break connection. Avoidance does.
3. You don't have to fix everything to heal trust. You just have to care enough to stay present.
4. Emotional safety is built when people know you'll still be there after the hard moments, not just during the easy ones.
5. Even imperfect repair attempts, done with sincerity, strengthen relationships more than silence or defensiveness ever could.
6. Real relationships aren't about getting it right every time. They're about returning to each other, again and again.

Self-Reflection

Take a few minutes to sit with these questions - in a journal, on a walk, or just quietly with yourself:

- When was the last time I chose to retreat instead of repair?
- What usually holds me back from reaching out after tension - fear, pride, uncertainty?
- What small repair attempt could I make today - even if it feels a little awkward?
- Who in my life consistently offers me repair, even in small ways? How does it impact the way I trust them?
- How would my relationships change if I stopped aiming for perfection - and started practicing small, steady repair instead?

Try This Strategy

The 24-Hour Repair Rule

Next time there's a bump - a misunderstanding, a harsh word, a weird silence - commit to making some kind of repair attempt within 24 hours.

It doesn't have to be a perfect apology. It could be:

A simple, "Hey, are we okay? I didn't love how we left that conversation."

A text that says, "Thinking about our conversation - just want you to know I care about you."

A voice memo: "I'm still processing, but I want to stay connected through this."

The point isn't to have it all figured out.

The point is to show that the relationship matters more than your pride.

Small, timely repair builds long-haul trust.

Conversation Starter

Want to invite more honest, caring relationships?

Try this brave check-in the next time you're with someone you trust:

"What's something I might accidentally do that makes you feel distant - and what helps you feel reconnected?"

(And be ready to share your own answers, too.)

You'll be amazed at what comes up - and how much closer it brings you.

CHAPTER 13

REPAIRING DISCONNECTION

HOW TO APOLOGIZE, REALIGN, AND RECONNECT WHEN THINGS GO OFF COURSE.

At some point in every meaningful relationship, professional or personal, disconnection happens. It may come from a miscommunication that was never fully clarified, a hurt feeling left unaddressed, or a gradual drift created by the chaos of life. Whatever the cause, one truth stands firm: it isn't the presence of disconnection that fractures trust. It's the absence of repair.

Emotional intelligence teaches us that repairing moments of tension is not about perfection, nor about preserving appearances. It's about honoring the relationship itself as a living, breathing entity that deserves care, even when caring feels inconvenient or uncomfortable. Left unattended, even small ruptures can deepen into misunderstandings that harden into distance. But when we respond with presence, vulnerability, and a willingness to engage - even imperfectly - we reinforce something far more powerful than flawless communication: we reinforce trust.

Research consistently shows that trust is built less through the avoidance of conflict and more through the ability to repair after it [10]. Yet in practice, repair is often where overthinking gets the loudest. We hesitate. We craft careful narratives. We wonder if reaching out will make things worse, if we are being too sensitive, if it's too late. This inner monologue can paralyze us, convincing us to retreat when the relationship actually needs us to lean in.

That's why understanding emotional repair is so crucial to sustaining meaningful connections. Repair is not about minimizing the hurt or forcing reconciliation on a rushed timeline. It's about staying relationally engaged even in discomfort. It's about acknowledging that trust isn't a one-time transaction - it's a living thread woven through small, ordinary moments where we choose to stay open rather than shut down.

Repair requires emotional literacy: the ability to recognize our own discomfort without letting it hijack the moment. It demands self-regulation: the maturity to tolerate feeling awkward, vulnerable, or exposed without immediately retreating into defensiveness. It draws on empathy: the capacity to prioritize the other person's experience without abandoning our own.

When we practice these skills, we send a profoundly human message:

"You matter to me more than my comfort. This connection matters to me more than my pride."

And that message, delivered consistently over time, is what strengthens relationships - not the absence of mistakes, but the presence of care after the inevitable messiness.

Repair isn't something that "nice" people do out of obligation.

It's a core emotional leadership skill.

It's a relational intelligence muscle.

It's the quiet architecture behind all the relationships we secretly admire - the ones that aren't perfect, but are undeniably resilient.

The good news is that repair doesn't require elaborate scripts or dramatic gestures.

It requires intention.

It requires humility.

And above all, it requires presence - the willingness to show up even when you're not sure how you'll be received.

Because here's the paradox:

It's not the hurt itself that most often breaks relationships.

It's the silence after the hurt.

It's the absence of acknowledgment.

It's the slow erosion of trust that happens when the relational "bruise" is never tended to, so it deepens into a wound.

Repair interrupts that erosion.

It tells the other person - and ourselves - that this connection is worth the awkwardness.

It's worth the courage.

It's worth the investment.

And over time, those small moments of intentional repair do something extraordinary:

They don't just heal individual moments of disconnection.

They build the kind of trust that can withstand the inevitable turbulence of real human relationships.

Repair doesn't guarantee instant resolution.

In fact, one of the most overlooked truths about relational repair is that its power lies not in producing immediate forgiveness, but in offering an open door. When we approach someone with a sincere acknowledgment of harm - whether real, perceived, or somewhere in between - we signal a willingness to hold space for complexity rather than demanding clarity or absolution on our preferred timeline.

Emotional intelligence research, especially the work of Dr. Marc Brackett at Yale's Center for Emotional Intelligence [35], shows that people are far more likely to respond positively to repair attempts when those attempts prioritize acknowledgment over explanation. In other words, people aren't looking for a perfect excuse. They're looking for evidence that their experience matters.

This is why phrases like, "I didn't mean to hurt you, but…" can unintentionally derail even the most well-intentioned repair. Defensiveness, even in small doses, shifts the focus away from connection and back onto personal preservation. It asks the injured person to manage our discomfort rather than giving them the room to process their own.

True repair resists that pull.

It stays low to the ground.

It stays close to the relational soil.

It sounds like:

"I realize what I said might have landed differently than I intended. I'm sorry for that."

or

"I can see that something between us shifted, and I want you to know I'm open to talking whenever you are ready."

There's no pushing.

No forcing.

Just presence.

Presence is the antidote to overthinking in repair moments.

Because when we're caught in our heads - rehearsing apologies, anticipating reactions, trying to "say it right" - we are no longer attuned to the person in front of us.

We're managing an internal performance, not participating in a shared moment of reconnection.

And reconnection only happens in the present, not in the perfect.

This is one of the reasons why people who seem "emotionally safe" aren't necessarily the most articulate or polished. They are the ones who stay open even when things are messy. They can sit with your hurt without rushing to fix it. They don't shame you for needing more time. They stay rooted in curiosity, not in control.

That's what repair asks of us: not mastery, but presence.

It's less about saying exactly the right thing and more about embodying the right posture - one of openness, care, and emotional spaciousness.

The truth is, emotional repair work mirrors physical healing in a profound way.

Just as a cut heals not from one grand gesture but from consistent, gentle care over time, relational wounds heal through consistent signals of safety, attention, and willingness.

Tiny deposits of trust.

Small recalibrations of connection.

Moment-by-moment choices to stay with, not away from, the discomfort.

And when we practice this kind of repair over time, something extraordinary happens:

We don't just heal the immediate hurt.

We create the kind of psychological safety that makes future misunderstandings less catastrophic.

We create relational elasticity - the ability to stretch without snapping.

That elasticity is the hallmark of resilient, lasting relationships.

Not because they never face tension.

But because they become places where tension doesn't have to equal rupture.

Where conflict doesn't immediately trigger abandonment.

Where care outweighs the need to be right.

In this way, learning how to repair becomes not just an interpersonal skill but a personal evolution.

It transforms the way we hold others, and the way we hold ourselves.

Because when you learn that mistakes don't have to be the end of connection…

You start to trust that your imperfections don't make you unlovable.

You start to trust that being human doesn't mean being disposable.

You start to live, and lead, with a different kind of courage.

The courage to stay.

The courage to soften.

The courage to repair.

Repairing relationships over time doesn't just strengthen the bond between people, it rewires our internal sense of security.

This matters more than we often realize.

Emotional intelligence isn't just about how we recognize and manage emotions in others, it's also about how we manage the emotions within ourselves when connection feels fragile.

Self-regulation, a key component of emotional intelligence identified by psychologist Daniel Goleman [36], is particularly critical during repair moments. Without it, even the most well-meaning attempts to reconnect can get hijacked by anxiety, shame, or defensiveness. Instead of staying grounded in the relationship, we spiral into self-protection.

But when we approach repair with self-regulation - anchoring ourselves in the intention to reconnect rather than the impulse to defend - we send a powerful signal to the other person:

"You are more important to me than my discomfort."

That signal, repeated over time, builds trust not through perfection, but through emotional safety.

Because here's the truth:

People don't stay connected to you because you never disappoint them.

They stay connected because they trust your heart to keep reaching for them even when you inevitably do.

When repair becomes a natural rhythm of your relationships, not a panicked response to emergencies, but an expected and welcome part of the connection, you create relational ecosystems where vulnerability can thrive.

And that changes everything.

It changes work cultures from brittle to resilient.

It changes friendships from surface-level to soul-deep.

It changes families from strained to strong.

It changes you, from someone who fears messing up, to someone who trusts themselves to make things right.

Repair teaches us that our worth isn't defined by whether we avoid mistakes.

It's revealed by how we meet them.

It's easy to admire people who seem effortlessly smooth in their relationships.

It's far more powerful, and far rarer, to become someone who is willing to be seen in the rough drafts.

To say, *"I messed up. And I'm here."*

To say, *"I care enough to stay awkward if it means staying connected."*

To say, *"I'm not perfect - but I'm still choosing you."*

That's the kind of presence that makes people breathe easier.

That invites honesty instead of performance.

That builds the kind of trust you can lean on when the inevitable storms of life come.

Because in the end, connection isn't about sealing every crack before it appears.

It's about becoming the kind of person who knows how to walk across the bridge - even when it trembles a little underfoot - and reach the other side with your heart intact.

Not flawless.

Not fearless.

But faithful to what matters most.

How to Know When Repair Is Needed

One of the quiet skills of emotionally intelligent people is the ability to notice the tiny shifts in connection before they turn into wide gaps.

Not because they're mind readers.

Not because they walk on eggshells.

But because they stay attuned to how presence feels between them and the people they care about.

Emotional intelligence researcher Dr. Marc Brackett, founder of the Yale Center for Emotional Intelligence, explains that tuning into the subtle emotional cues of others, and ourselves, is what allows us to intervene early, before disconnection hardens [35].

The early signs that a relationship needs a small repair are rarely dramatic.

They're the awkward silences after something sensitive is said.

The slight withdrawal you notice in a text thread that used to be lively.

The way someone's responses get a little shorter, a little cooler.

The way you yourself start overthinking before reaching out again.

Most of the time, we sense it in our bodies first.

A tightening.

A hesitation.

An internal ping of, "Something feels a little off."

And our instinct is often to ignore it.

To tell ourselves, "It's nothing," "I'm being dramatic," or "It'll fix itself."

But emotional intelligence teaches us that relationships thrive when we stay responsive to these micro-signals, not suspicious, not paranoid, but gently curious.

When you sense a little drift, the bravest thing you can do isn't to pull away to protect yourself.

It's to lean in.

To reach out, not with an accusation, not with a demand, but with an open-hearted check-in:

"Hey, I might be overthinking this, but I feel like something's been a little off. How are you really doing?"

Notice how the framing matters.

You're not saying, *"You're mad at me, aren't you?"*

You're saying, "I care about this enough to notice. And I care about you enough to ask."

That tiny move - naming the disconnection without dramatizing it - often creates a huge wave of relief in the other person.

Because chances are, they felt the drift too.

And they were waiting, hoping, for someone to make it safe to name it.

Every time you do that - every time you refuse to let a tiny crack widen into a canyon - you become a bridge builder.

Someone people feel safe around.

Someone people trust, not because you never mess up, but because you keep choosing the relationship over your ego.

And that kind of presence is unforgettable.

Making a Repair Attempt Without Making It Weird

Once you sense a small drift, the next question is often:

"Okay… but what do I actually say?"

This is where overthinking loves to creep in.

You start spiraling:

What if I'm imagining the distance?

What if bringing it up makes it worse?

What if they don't even care that things feel off?

Pause.

Breathe.

Remember: the goal of repair isn't to force a confession, extract an apology, or script a perfect conversation.

The goal is simply to reopen the door.

A repair attempt doesn't have to be deep or dramatic.

In fact, the lighter and more genuine it is, the safer it feels.

Sometimes, the best repair attempts sound almost ordinary:

"Hey, just realizing we haven't caught up in a bit. How are you?"

"I was thinking about our last conversation and wondering how you're feeling."

"Can we grab coffee soon? I miss hearing what's going on with you."

Notice:

You're not accusing.

You're not assuming.

You're inviting.

You're choosing curiosity over assumption.

Care over control.

And you're sending a powerful emotional signal:

"I value this connection enough to notice. And I care enough to stay open, even if it feels a little awkward."

Neuroscience backs up why this matters.

According to Dr. Matthew Lieberman's research on social cognition, our brains are wired to interpret small gestures of social reengagement as profound signals of safety [2].

Even brief, casual bids for reconnection lower stress hormones and increase feelings of belonging.

That means:

- Your simple check-in text? Calms someone's nervous system.
- Your casual, "Miss seeing you around" comment? Sparks trust.
- Your willingness to stay open, even when it feels uncertain? Changes the emotional climate.

And here's the truth:

Most people aren't longing for you to say the perfect thing.

They're longing to know you care enough to say something.

When you make a repair attempt, even a slightly awkward one, you're saying:

"You're more important to me than my pride."

And whether or not they can respond perfectly in return, that message lands.

It matters.

It lingers.

It builds trust in the places words alone can't reach.

Of course, not every repair attempt is met with instant warmth.

Sometimes you'll reach out and get a polite but distant reply.

Sometimes you'll get no reply at all.

And it's tempting - so tempting - to take that silence or coolness as proof that you were wrong to reach out.

That you messed up.

That the connection isn't worth trying for.

But here's something emotional intelligence teaches us:

Other people's reactions aren't always about us.

In fact, they often aren't.

Someone might be carrying their own shame, hurt, busyness, or fear.

Someone might have grown up in a culture or family where direct repair wasn't modeled, and they genuinely don't know how to respond.

Someone might desperately want to reconnect, but feel paralyzed by their own overthinking too.

This is why resilience matters.

This is why emotional agility matters.

Dr. Susan David's research on emotional agility reminds us that the ability to stay rooted in our values - even when our emotions get messy - is a key predictor of strong, meaningful relationships [37].

If your value is connection, not control, you can offer a bid for repair without needing it to go a certain way.

You can say, "I miss you" without needing them to say "I miss you too."

You can invite, without demanding.

You can stay open, even when it feels vulnerable.

Because real connection isn't built by controlling outcomes.

It's built by showing up real.

Overthinking makes it about winning or losing:

Did they text back fast enough?

Did they match my effort?

Did they make me feel instantly reassured?

Presence makes it about staying in alignment with who you want to be:

Did I reach out because I care?

Did I stay kind even when it felt a little raw?

Did I honor my value of connection, even without guarantees?

When you anchor yourself in presence instead of performance, you stop trying to manage the uncontrollable.

You stay true to yourself.

You build trust, even when the outcome is uncertain, because you trust yourself to show up the way you want to show up.

And here's the secret most people miss:

The relationship that changes most when you do this?

It's not just the one with the other person.

It's the one with yourself.

Every time you lean into care over comfort…

Every time you offer connection over control…

Every time you stay, even when your ego screams to retreat…

You build a deeper, steadier relationship with your own heart.

You prove to yourself:

I'm someone who chooses love over fear.

I'm someone who stays real, even when it's messy.

I'm someone I can trust to show up true.

And that inner trust?

It changes everything.

Because once you start showing up in this way - anchored, steady, willing - you start to realize something:

You don't have to try harder to build deeper trust.

You just have to stay softer longer.

You don't have to engineer deeper connection by crafting the perfect text, orchestrating the perfect conversation, or endlessly rehearsing what to say.

You just have to keep weaving small, human moments into the relationship, strand by strand, without needing instant proof that it's "working."

This is what Dr. Carol Dweck's research on growth mindset teaches us [14]:

Growth, whether in skills, resilience, or relationships, isn't about dramatic leaps.

It's about tiny, repeated actions taken consistently over time, especially when no immediate payoff is visible.

It's believing in the slow process.

The same way a muscle strengthens from repeated reps that don't feel like much in the moment.

The same way a plant grows, imperceptibly, from tiny sips of sunlight and water.

Relationships, too, deepen through small, cumulative trust deposits:

- Answering the text, even when you're tired.
- Following up after a hard conversation, even when you feel awkward.

- Remembering something important to them, even when you're busy.

Not because you're trying to "earn" their affection.

But because connection is who you are.

When you lead this way, from authenticity, not strategy, trust becomes less about winning someone's approval and more about witnessing the relationship unfold naturally.

Some relationships will deepen.

Some will plateau.

Some will drift.

That's not failure.

That's life.

Your job isn't to force every connection into intimacy.

Your job is to stay faithful to your intention:

To be someone who shows up.

To be someone who sees.

To be someone who keeps choosing connection over fear.

And when you live that way, your life quietly fills with something richer than surface-level networking ever could offer:

Real belonging.

Not just being known for your role or your achievements.

Not just being liked for what you can offer.

But being trusted, deeply, consistently, imperfectly, for who you are.

And it all starts by choosing, moment after moment, to stop overthinking connection…

…and start building it, one small, real act at a time.

STOP OVERTHINKING IT

PAUSE. REFLECT. APPLY.

What to Remember

1. Deep trust isn't built through grand gestures - it's layered quietly through small, repeated moments of care.
2. Emotional intelligence isn't about mastering the perfect reaction. It's about staying attuned to another person's emotional landscape, even when things get messy.
3. Connection deepens not because you never miss a beat, but because you notice when you do - and you return.
4. You don't need to script every interaction. You need to stay present enough to notice the openings for real relationship - and step through them, even imperfectly.
5. Relationships thrive on responsiveness, not perfection. The faster you notice and respond to disconnection, the stronger the emotional bond becomes.

Self-Reflection

- Take a few moments - right now if you can - and ask yourself:
- Where in my relationships am I still operating like trust is a one-time achievement, instead of an ongoing practice?
- When was the last time I noticed a small opportunity to deepen a connection - and did I act on it, or hesitate?
- What stories do I tell myself when a relationship feels quieter than usual? (Do I assume disinterest, or do I stay curious?)
- Who in my life models emotional responsiveness, and what can I learn from the way they show up?
- What would happen if I gave myself permission to be a beginner at repair, focusing on presence over perfection?

Try This Strategy

The Micro-Moment Check-In

Each day this week, challenge yourself to notice - and act on - one small opportunity for connection.

Maybe it's:

Sending a "thinking of you" text without overthinking the wording.

Following up with someone you've been meaning to check in with - even if it's been a while.

Asking a deeper question when someone mentions something in passing ("How's that been feeling for you lately?").

Simply saying, *"Hey, I realized I was a little distracted earlier - I'm sorry about that. You're important to me."*

Not big.

Not dramatic.

Not performative.

Just one micro-moment of presence.

One stitch in the fabric of trust.

(And watch what starts to happen - not overnight, but over time.)

Conversation Starter

Want to strengthen an important relationship - or rekindle one that's gone a little quiet?

Try this invitation:

"I've been thinking lately about how easy it is to lose touch - and how much I value the realness we have. What's something small that helps you feel connected to people in your life?"

No pressure. No fixing. Just a gentle, open-handed way to spark a deeper, realer dialogue — one that invites connection, not performance.

Because trust doesn't grow in the highlight reel.

It grows in the messy, beautiful, real middle.

Chapter 14

You Belong Here

Creating space for yourself and others to thrive in relationships - without overthinking it.

There's a quiet ache that hums beneath so many of our interactions - a silent, persistent question: Do I belong here?

Not just "Am I included?"

Not just "Did they invite me?"

But deeper: Am I seen for who I really am? Am I valued when I'm not performing?

Belonging is one of the most fundamental human needs. According to psychologist Abraham Maslow's original hierarchy of needs [38], right after our basic survival needs like food and shelter comes love and belonging. It's as essential to our well-being as breathing. Yet, in a culture obsessed with achievement, image, and speed, many of us are left feeling like belonging is something we have to earn rather than something we already deserve.

When we overthink our relationships, when we second-guess our value, when we edit ourselves to fit the perceived expectations of others, we don't actually create more belonging. We create more distance. We armor up. We trade authenticity for approval. And even when we "succeed" - even when we are included - we still feel the ache. Because deep down, we know they don't see the real us. They see the version we thought we needed to become in order to belong.

The antidote to this isn't trying harder to fit in.

It's learning to stay rooted in who you are - even when the fear of not belonging tries to hijack your brain.

Dr. Brené Brown, whose research on belonging has deeply reshaped our understanding of connection, reminds us that true belonging doesn't require us to change who we are - it requires us to be who we are [39]. That's a radical shift. It means that belonging starts not with external validation, but with internal acceptance. It means creating a space within yourself that says: I'm worthy of connection exactly as I am.

And here's where emotional intelligence comes in.

Self-awareness - the first pillar of emotional intelligence - teaches us to recognize when we're slipping into performance. It teaches us to catch the subtle moments when we're armoring up, playing a role, or shrinking to stay safe. The more self-aware we become, the more we can notice, Ah, there's that old fear again, and gently redirect ourselves back toward authenticity.

But belonging isn't just about self-acceptance. It's about creating spaces where others can feel that way too.

It's about being the person who notices when someone's standing awkwardly at the edge of the group and inviting them in, not because they performed perfectly, but because they're human.

It's about being the coworker who values the quiet contributor as much as the outspoken one.

It's about being the friend who says, "You don't have to impress me. I'm already glad you're here."

Belonging multiplies when we offer it - without conditions.

And ironically, the more we focus on cultivating spaces where others feel they belong, the more we feel it ourselves.

Because belonging isn't a prize.

It's a practice.

It's not a stamp you earn once and carry forever.

It's a choice you make again and again: to show up real, to stay soft when you want to harden, to be the kind of person who reminds others (and yourself) that worth isn't performance-based.

You don't belong because you're polished.

You don't belong because you're impressive.

You belong because you're human.

And the world needs more of that kind of belonging.

Not curated.

Not conditional.

Not earned.

Real.

Messy.

Alive.

Thriving in relationships doesn't mean always getting it right. It doesn't mean managing every conversation flawlessly, predicting every emotional nuance, or perfecting your timing so you never miss a beat.

Thriving means something quieter. It means feeling safe enough to be your full, real self - and making it safe for others to do the same.

Emotional intelligence teaches us that thriving relationships are not about emotional perfection. They are about emotional presence. Dr. Daniel Goleman, who popularized the concept of emotional intelligence, emphasized that one of the strongest predictors of relational success is not how well we perform emotional "tasks," but how well we stay in emotional connection [16].

This is vital, because when we overthink every interaction, when we scan for signs we're doing it wrong, when we replay conversations like a highlight reel of mistakes, we pull away from presence. We stop being with people, and start performing for them. And ironically, the harder we work to "get it right," the more disconnected we feel.

The key to thriving isn't mastering every social cue. It's learning how to recover when we inevitably miss one. It's trusting that a relationship can survive an awkward silence, a clumsy word, a slow text response - and that you can survive it too.

The most alive relationships - the ones where people actually flourish, are messy. They're human. They are full of missed cues and honest repairs, laughter that spills into the gaps, hard conversations that forge deeper understanding, silences that aren't scary because the connection underneath is strong.

Thriving, then, isn't about managing relationships perfectly.

It's about living them imperfectly, but wholeheartedly.

When you stop overthinking your belonging, you stop performing your life.

You start living it.

You walk into rooms without carrying a list of ways you need to prove yourself. You reach out to people because you care, not because you calculated it would make you look good.

You speak your truth even if your voice shakes a little. You stay present when the conversation gets messy instead of mentally exiting to craft the perfect response.

And people feel it.

They trust it.

Because it's rare.

In a world conditioned to prize performance, presence is radical.

And it's healing.

It softens the armor we all wear.

It invites others into the safety of real human connection.

It reminds people - in the smallest, quietest ways - that they belong, too.

This is why building belonging, both for yourself and others, is one of the most transformational things you can do. It's not a side effect of connection.

It's the soil connection grows from.

When people feel they belong, they risk showing up more authentically.

They contribute more freely.

They forgive more quickly.

They stay more faithfully.

In workplaces, teams with high levels of psychological safety - the feeling that you can take risks, be vulnerable, and still belong - outperform teams that rely on fear, competition, or constant evaluation [9].

In friendships, belonging creates the freedom to grow and change without fear that your evolution will cost you your community.

In families, belonging gives space for mistakes, messiness, and healing love, not just pride or performance.

In every corner of our lives, belonging is the deep hum beneath thriving.

And here's the part that most people miss:

You don't create belonging by controlling how you're perceived.

You create belonging by being, not by managing.

You create belonging when you listen without an agenda.

When you give someone space to not be polished or "on."

When you let your own guard down first, quietly signaling:

You don't have to earn your way into this conversation.

You're already welcome here.

You also create belonging for yourself when you stop waiting for someone else to hand it to you. When you decide - in your own mind, your own body, your own being - "I belong because I am human. I belong because I am here. I don't have to overperform for it, and I don't have to shrink for it either."

That internal shift changes everything.

Because the moment you stop overthinking whether you belong, you start showing up in a way that naturally makes space for deeper connection.

You walk into the room differently.

You listen differently.

You are different - not because you became something you weren't, but because you dropped something you never needed to carry.

You dropped the self-surveillance.

The performance anxiety.

The endless second-guessing.

And what rises in its place is something steadier.

Something softer.

Something magnetic.

Real connection always starts with presence, and presence always starts with self-acceptance.

You don't have to master every social skill.

You don't have to be the funniest, smartest, most dazzling person in the room.

You just have to stay.

Stay open.

Stay curious.

Stay real.

And trust that's enough.

The truth is, spaces don't become safe because the right people show up. Spaces become safe because people choose to show up in a way that makes safety possible.

And you have that power.

Every time you smile first.

Every time you assume positive intent.

Every time you make room for a messy answer instead of a polished one.

Every time you let someone feel seen without making them perform for it.

You're weaving a culture of belonging - strand by intentional strand.

And when you do that, you're not just creating a space where they can thrive.

You're creating a space where you can thrive, too.

Because belonging is mutual.

It's not something you hustle for.

It's something you nurture - moment by moment, interaction by interaction, relationship by relationship.

When you stop overthinking how you're perceived...

When you stop shrinking or shape-shifting to "fit"...

When you root yourself in the quiet knowing that "I am enough, and others are enough too"...

You become the invitation.

You become the person whose presence makes other people breathe easier.

You become the kind of leader, friend, teammate, human that others feel better around - not because you dazzled them, but because you saw them.

Because you stayed with them.

Because you made the room softer, braver, more honest, just by being willing to bring your whole self.

That's how real belonging is built.

But here's the part nobody tells you:

Belonging doesn't come with a flashing neon sign.

It's quiet. Subtle. Felt more than declared.

It's in the way your shoulders relax around someone who asks how you really are and waits for the unpolished answer. It's in the way you laugh a little louder, risk a little more honesty, dream a little bigger, because someone else's presence makes it feel safe to be seen. And when you create spaces like that - when you choose to lead with presence, with care, with realness - you change more than just a moment. You change lives.

You change the story someone tells themselves about whether they matter. You change the script they've been handed about needing to hustle for love, compete for worthiness, or perform for acceptance. You remind them, and yourself, that connection was never meant to be a contest. It was meant to be a coming home.

I didn't always know this. For a long time, I thought belonging was about becoming what each new environment wanted me to be. When you change schools 33 times before adulthood, you get good at scanning a room and figuring out how to blend. How to shape-shift just enough to avoid rejection. You learn to anticipate the right answers, the right posture, the right way to laugh at the right time.

But what you don't learn - what you can't learn when you're always performing - is how to be truly known.

And you can't feel you belong if you're hiding half of yourself.

It took me decades - and a lot of heartache - to unlearn the survival strategies that kept me safe, but also kept me small. It took walking away from spaces where I was praised for fitting in but never felt seen for who I really was. It took daring to believe that I didn't have to out-perform loneliness - I could heal it by standing still and letting myself be loved as I already was.

It took seeing how even in my professional life - in conference ballrooms, boardrooms, community events - the real magic always happened the same way:

When someone dropped the script.

When someone dared to be human.

One of the most unexpected moments of belonging happened in Champlain, Illinois, during a multi-day leadership training I delivered for a group of Army professionals.

The training coordinator - a woman I'd never met before - took me to lunch. She had planned a different local spot for us to try, which in itself was kind. But what made those lunches memorable wasn't the food. It was the way she showed up. Not just as a logistical contact or a coordinator checking boxes - but as a person, willing to connect.

On one of our drives, she told me about her childhood love for Nancy Drew books. The way her eyes lit up, the fondness in her voice, the detail with which she described scouring used bookstores to now find copies for her daughter - who had inherited the same love - it sparked something in me. That same love had lived in my childhood too.

It was such a simple moment. A shared memory. A soft place in both our stories where something familiar and joyful lived.

Later that evening, I wandered into a used bookstore across from my hotel. And there they were - spines of yellow, a few worn covers, titles I hadn't seen in decades. I picked up a handful and brought them to her the next morning.

Her face lit up. Not because they were expensive or rare - but because she felt seen. Understood. Remembered.

That's what belonging looks like. Not grand gestures. Not perfect words. Just the quiet generosity of presence. The willingness to notice someone's joy and reflect it back to them.

To this day, every time I see a Nancy Drew book tucked into the shelf of a thrift store or buried in the corner of an antique shop, I think of her. And I smile. Because that's what belonging does - it leaves a thread. A warmth. A human memory that tells you: You mattered here.

And that's the thing about belonging. It doesn't always arrive with fanfare. Sometimes it shows up in the form of an old book. A conversation in a car. A moment when someone sees your joy and joins you in it.

You don't have to plan it. You just have to be open enough to notice it.

And sometimes, when you do, you help someone else feel like they're not just in the room - they belong there.

In all my years working with leaders, teams, and individuals across industries, one truth rises above the noise:

Where belonging grows, everything else grows too.

Teams with a culture of belonging outperform their peers by over 56% in productivity and innovation [40].

Students who feel a sense of belonging are four times more likely to persist through challenges and graduate [41].

Individuals with high social connection report lower rates of anxiety, depression, and chronic disease [1].

Belonging isn't a "nice to have."

It's the foundation of thriving - personally, professionally, relationally.

And yet, so many of us are starving for it because we're too busy trying to earn what was always meant to be shared.

We've been taught that belonging is transactional:

"Be impressive enough, and you'll be accepted."

"Be polished enough, and you'll be safe."

But the real truth?

Belonging can't be bought or bartered.

It can only be built - from the inside out.

And it starts by deciding:

I will not shrink to belong.

I will not shape-shift to survive.

I will not overthink myself out of connection.

I will belong by bringing my real self to the table - not my curated, performative, overworked self - but my honest, messy, human self.

And when you show up like that?

You invite others to do the same.

You don't just find belonging.

You create it.

And you create it everywhere you go - in your work, in your friendships, in your family, in the chance meetings on a shuttle bus, on a first-class flight to a conference, in line for coffee, across tables and across years.

You become a builder of spaces where people can finally, safely exhale and say: "I belong here. I am enough."

And you get to feel it too.

Because that's the most beautiful part:

When you create belonging for others,

you create it for yourself.

And that, my friend - that is the real revolution.

Not a revolution of performance.

But a revolution of presence, compassion, and belonging.

A connection revolution.

The Quiet Revolution Starts Here

You made it.

Not just to the last page - but to a new beginning.

Because if you've read this far, you're not just interested in connection.

You're ready to live it.

Not perfectly.

Not performatively.

But bravely, imperfectly, humanly.

You're ready to be the kind of person who shows up - real and present - in a world that's starving for it.

You're ready to build trust one conversation at a time.

To choose presence over polish.

To stop overthinking your worth.

To create belonging without waiting for permission.

That's not small work.

That's revolutionary work.

And it starts right where you are - with the next relationship you nurture, the next stranger you smile at, the next vulnerable moment you stay for instead of retreating from.

You don't need a bigger platform.

You don't need a fancier title.

You don't need permission.

You have everything you need already:

Your humanity.

Your presence.

Your willingness to show up real.

That's how the revolution spreads - quietly, powerfully, inevitably.

One brave moment of connection at a time.

And if you ever start to doubt it - if you ever wonder if it matters, if it's working, if you're making a difference - remember this:

Every time you choose presence over performance, every time you let someone feel seen, every time you dare to stay real - you are changing the world.

You are the revolution.

And it's just beginning.

Author's Note

Thank you for spending this time with me.

Writing this book wasn't just about sharing ideas - it was about building a bridge.

A reminder that we're not alone in wanting deeper connection, more meaning, and real belonging.

If something here sparked something in you - a new thought, a little more courage, a quiet yes - I hope you'll carry it forward in your own way, in your own spaces.

And if you'd like to stay connected, you're warmly invited to join me at [insert your website or social media handle here].

The conversation - the revolution - is just getting started.

Stay real. Stay open. Stay human.

We need you.

With gratitude,

Dr. Jolene Church

REFERENCES

1. U.S. Department of Health and Human Services. *Our Epidemic of Loneliness and Isolation: The U.S. Surgeon General's Advisory on the Healing Effects of Social Connection and Community.* 2023.

2. Lieberman, Matthew D. *Social: Why Our Brains Are Wired to Connect.* Crown Publishers, 2013.

3. Todd, A. R., Berry Mendes, W., Galinsky, A. D. (2011). *Perspective taking combats automatic expressions of racial bias.* Journal of Personality and Social Psychology, 100(6), 1027–1042. https://doi.org/10.1037/a0022308

4. Huang, K., Yeomans, M., Brooks, A. W., Minson, J. A., & Gino, F. (2017). *It doesn't hurt to ask: Question-asking increases liking.* Journal: Social Psychological and Personality Science, 8(3), 233–241. https://doi.org/10.1177/1948550616667456

5. Rozovsky, J. (2015). *The five keys to a successful Google team.* Google re:Work. Retrieved from https://rework.withgoogle.com/blog/five-keys-to-a-successful-google-team/

6. Garton, E., & Mankins, M. (2020). *Authenticity matters more than charisma.* Harvard Business Review. Retrieved from https://hbr.org/2020/06/authenticity-matters-more-than-charisma

7. Brown, B. (2018). *Dare to Lead: Brave Work. Tough Conversations. Whole Hearts.* New York: Random House.

8. Brown, B. (2010). *The Gifts of Imperfection: Let Go of Who You Think You're Supposed to Be and Embrace Who You Are.* Center City, MN: Hazelden Publishing.

9. Edmondson, A. (1999). "Psychological Safety and Learning Behavior in Work Teams." *Administrative Science Quarterly,* 44(2), 350–383.

10. Gottman, J. M., & Silver, N. (1999). *The Seven Principles for Making Marriage Work.* Crown.

11. Harter, J. K., Schmidt, F. L., & Hayes, T. L. (2002). *Business-unit-level relationship between employee satisfaction, employee engagement, and business outcomes: A meta-analysis.* Journal of Applied Psychology, 87(2), 268–279. https://doi.org/10.1037/0021-9010.87.2.268

12. *Gallup. (2023). State of the Global Workplace: 2023 Report. Gallup. https://www.gallup.com/workplace/349484/state-of-the-global-workplace.aspx*

13. Kumar, A., & Epley, N. (2022). The surprise of reaching out: Appreciated more than we think. *Journal of Personality and Social Psychology, 123*(4), 513–528. https://doi.org/10.1037/pspi0000402

14. Dweck, Carol S. *Mindset: The New Psychology of Success.* Ballantine Books, 2006.

15. Barsade, S. G., & O'Neill, O. A. (2014). *What's love got to do with it? A longitudinal study of the culture of companionate love and employee and client outcomes in a long-term care setting.* Administrative Science Quarterly, 59(4), 551–598. https://doi.org/10.1177/0001839214538636

16. Goleman, D. (2006). *Social Intelligence: The New Science of Human Relationships.* Bantam Books.

17. Cuddy, A., Kohut, M., & Neffinger, J. (2013). *Connect, then lead.* Harvard Business Review, 91(7/8), 54–61.

18. Porges, S. W. (2011). *The polyvagal theory: Neurophysiological foundations of emotions, attachment, communication, self-regulation.* W.W. Norton & Company.

19. BetterUp. (2019). *The value of belonging at work: New research on the missing piece of your diversity, equity & inclusion strategy.* BetterUp Labs. https://www.betterup.com/resources/blog/belonging-at-work

20. Zenger, J., & Folkman, J. (2022, September 7). *The small things that make employees feel appreciated.* Harvard Business Review. https://hbr.org/2022/09/the-small-things-that-make-employees-feel-appreciated

21. Rozovsky, J. (2015). *The five keys to a successful Google team.* re:Work by Google. Retrieved from https://rework.withgoogle.com/blog/five-keys-to-a-successful-google-team/

22. Casciaro, T., Gino, F., & Kouchaki, M. (2016). *Learn to love networking.* Harvard Business Review. Retrieved from https://hbr.org/2016/05/learn-to-love-networking

23. Zhao, X., Epley, N., & Kumar, A. (2022). *The surprising power of simply asking: Underestimating the positive impact of kindness on others. Emotion*, 22(4), 543–548. https://doi.org/10.1037/emo0001005

24. Waldinger, R. J., & Schulz, M. S. (2023). *The Good Life: Lessons from the World's Longest Scientific Study of Happiness.* Simon & Schuster.

25. Holt-Lunstad, J., Smith, T. B., & Layton, J. B. (2010). Social relationships and mortality risk: A meta-analytic review. *PLoS Medicine, 7*(7), e1000316. https://doi.org/10.1371/journal.pmed.1000316

26. Epley, N., & Schroeder, J. (2014). Mistakenly seeking solitude. *Journal of Experimental Psychology: General, 143*(5), 1980–1999. https://doi.org/10.1037/a0037323

27. Brown, B. (2012). Daring greatly: How the courage to be vulnerable transforms the way we live, love, parent, and lead. Gotham Books.

28. Pentland, A. (2012). The new science of building great teams. Harvard Business Review, 90(4), 60–69.

29. Edmondson, A. C. (2019). *The Fearless Organization: Creating Psychological Safety in the Workplace for Learning, Innovation, and Growth.* Wiley.

30. Gottman, J. M., & Silver, N. (2011). *What Makes Love Last?: How to Build Trust and Avoid Betrayal.* Simon & Schuster.

31. Johnson, S. (2008). *Hold Me Tight: Seven Conversations for a Lifetime of Love.* Little, Brown Spark.

32. Tronick, E. Z., Als, H., Adamson, L., Wise, S., & Brazelton, T. B. (1978). The infant's response to entrapment between contradictory messages in face-to-face interaction. *Journal of the American Academy of Child Psychiatry, 17*(1), 1–13. https://doi.org/10.1016/S0002-7138(09)62273-1

33. Kramer, R. M., & Lewicki, R. J. (2010). Repairing and enhancing trust: Approaches to reducing organizational trust deficits. *The Academy of Management Annals, 4*(1), 245–277. https://doi.org/10.1080/19416520.2010.487403

34. Zaki, J., & Ochsner, K. N. (2012). The neuroscience of empathy: progress, pitfalls and promise. *Nature Neuroscience, 15*(5), 675–680. https://doi.org/10.1038/nn.3085

35. Brackett, M. A. (2019). *Permission to feel: Unlocking the power of emotions to help our kids, ourselves, and our society thrive.* Celadon Books.

36. Goleman, D. (1995). *Emotional intelligence: Why it can matter more than IQ.* Bantam Books.

37. David, S. (2016). *Emotional agility: Get unstuck, embrace change, and thrive in work and life.* Avery.

38. Maslow, A. H. (1943). A theory of human motivation. *Psychological Review, 50*(4), 370–396. https://doi.org/10.1037/h0054346

39. Brown, B. (2017). *Braving the wilderness: The quest for true belonging and the courage to stand alone.* Random House.

40. BetterUp. (2021). *The value of belonging at work: A report by BetterUp Labs.* https://www.betterup.com/resources/research/value-of-belonging-at-work

41. Strayhorn, T. L. (2018). *College students' sense of belonging: A key to educational success for all students* (2nd ed.). Routledge.

42. Delizonna, Laura. "High-Performing Teams Need Psychological Safety. Here's How to Create It." *Harvard Business Review*, August 24, 2017.

43. Pentland, Alex. *Social Physics: How Good Ideas Spread – The Lessons from a New Science.* Penguin Press, 2014. (MIT Human Dynamics Lab)

44. Gottman, John, and Nan Silver. *The Seven Principles for Making Marriage Work.* Harmony Books, 1999.

45. Edmondson, Amy C. *The Fearless Organization: Creating Psychological Safety in the Workplace for Learning, Innovation, and Growth.* Wiley, 2018.

46. Brown, Brené. *Dare to Lead: Brave Work. Tough Conversations. Whole Hearts.* Random House, 2018.

47. Dweck, Carol S., and Walton, Gregory M. "The Psychology of Trust and its Role in Relationship Repair." Stanford Strengths-Based Leadership Lab, 2022.

48. Stanford Social Neuroscience Lab. Research on vulnerability-based trust and social risk pathways. Stanford University, 2022.

49. Gottman, John, and Nan Silver. *The Science of Trust: Emotional Attunement for Couples.* Norton, 2011.

50. Maslow, Abraham H. *Motivation and Personality.* Harper and Row, 1954.

51. Brown, Brené. *Braving the Wilderness: The Quest for True Belonging and the Courage to Stand Alone.* Random House, 2017.

52. Goleman, Daniel. *Emotional Intelligence: Why It Can Matter More Than IQ.* Bantam Books, 1995.

53. Edmondson, Amy C. "Psychological Safety, Trust, and Learning in Organizations: A Group-Level Lens." *Academy of Management Journal*, vol. 44, no. 2, 1999, pp. 350-367.

54. Deloitte. *The Diversity and Inclusion Revolution: Eight Powerful Truths.* Deloitte Insights, 2018.

55. Stanford Center for Opportunity Policy in Education (SCOPE). *Learning to Belong: The Importance of School Belonging for Students' Outcomes.* 2019.

56. U.S. Department of Health and Human Services. *Our Epidemic of Loneliness and Isolation: The U.S. Surgeon General's Advisory on the Healing Effects of Social Connection and Community.* 2023.

57. Strayhorn, T. L. (2012). College Students' Sense of Belonging: A Key to Educational Success for All Students. Routledge.

58. Abraham Maslow. (1943). A Theory of Human Motivation. Psychological Review.

59. Stanford University Strengths-Based Leadership Lab. (2021). Trust, Repair, and Relational Resilience: New Insights from Strengths-Based Leadership Research. (Study summary and white paper.)

60. Stanford Social Neuroscience Lab. (2020). Emotional Risk and Social Connection: Neural Pathways of Vulnerability. Stanford Research Brief.

61. Edward Tronick. (1978). Still-Face Paradigm. Harvard Medical School Center on the Developing Child.

62. Dr. Sue Johnson. (2008). Hold Me Tight: Seven Conversations for a Lifetime of Love. Little, Brown Spark.

63. Journal of Social and Personal Relationships. (2023). Everyday Interaction and Relational Closeness: A Longitudinal Study.

About the Author

Dr. Jolene Church is a workplace culture whisperer, bestselling author, executive coach, and the founder of DJC Consulting, Coaching & Training. With a doctorate in organizational leadership and over two decades of experience transforming teams and organizations, Dr. Church is known for helping people feel seen, heard, and valued - whether in boardrooms, break rooms, or the middle of burnout.

She has trained and coached leaders across government agencies, Fortune 500 companies, nonprofits, and universities, equipping them with the tools to lead with emotional intelligence, authenticity, and courage.

When she's not delivering keynotes, running leadership intensives, or training federal agencies on how to build cultures of belonging, you'll find her walking her rescue dog, Finn, mentoring fellow leaders, or writing her next book.

Let's stay connected:

- 🌐 www.drjolenechurch.com
- ✉️ Join the Connection Revolution newsletter
- 🎤 Book Dr. Church to speak: info@drjolenechurch.com
- 📱 Follow on LinkedIn, Instagram, TikTok @drjolenechurch

www.ingramcontent.com/pod-product-compliance
Lightning Source LLC
Chambersburg PA
CBHW070634160426
43194CB00009B/1458